WIESEL, WIESENTHAL, KLARSFELD

The Holocaust Survivors

Tabatha Yeatts

Enslow Publishers, Inc.

40 Industrial Road
Box 398
Berkeley Heights, NJ 07922
USA

http://www.enslow.com

This book is dedicated with love and appreciation to my family:
my husband, Ben
my daughter, Ariana
my parents, Harry Jr. and Catherine
my grandparents, Harry Sr. and Helen

Originally published as *The Holocaust Survivors* in 1998.

Library of Congress Cataloging-in-Publication Data

Yeatts, Tabatha, author.
  Wiesel, Wiesenthal, Klarsfeld : the Holocaust survivors / Tabatha Yeatts.
    pages cm — (Remembering the Holocaust)
  Includes bibliographical references and index.
  Summary: "Discusses the experiences of people who survived the Holocaust, the trials of Nazi
leaders at Nuremberg, the establishment of the state of Israel, the search for justice, and efforts of
the survivors to begin new lives"—Provided by publisher.
    ISBN 978-0-7660-6202-3
    1. Holocaust survivors—Juvenile literature. 2. Jews—History—1945—Juvenile literature.
  3. Jews—Europe—History—20th century—Juvenile literature. I. Title.
    DS135.E83Y38 2014
    940.53'18—dc23
                                                                    2014007029

Future Editions:
Paperback ISBN: 978-0-7660-6203-0
EPUB ISBN: 978-0-7660-6204-7
Single-User PDF ISBN: 978-0-7660-6205-4
Multi-User PDF ISBN: 978-0-7660-6206-1

Printed in the United States of America
072014 HF Group, North Manchester, IN
10 9 8 7 6 5 4 3 2 1

Illustration Credits: Enslow Publishers, Inc, pp. 8, 35; National Archives, p. 1; National Archives, Washington, D.C., courtesy of USHMM photo archives, pp. 40, 51.

Cover Illustration: National Archives and Records Administration (NARA): Wobbelin Concentration Camp, recently captured by troops of the 82nd Airborne Division. Many prisoners were found nearly starved to death. Here former prisoners are being taken to a hospital for medical attention. Germany, May 4, 1945. Photographer: Pvt. Ralph Forney, U.S. Army

CONTENTS

✹⟞ ACKNOWLEDGMENTS ⟶✹

I would like to thank Alex Gross; Sylvia Wygoda of the Georgia Commission on the Holocaust; Sandy Berman of the William Breman Jewish Heritage Museum; Leslie Swift and Genya Markon of the United States Holocaust Memorial Museum Photograph Archives; Charles Ferree; Anthony Belmonte; Steven Fransblow; Sam Arbiser; Jacob Kahan; Stanley Lefco; The Simon Wiesenthal Center; and Edita Bielavska for their assistance with this project.

> All men and women are born, live, suffer and die. . . . We do not choose to be born. We do not choose our parents. We do not choose our historical epoch, the country of our birth, or the immediate circumstances of our upbringing. We do not, most of us, choose to die; nor do we choose the time and conditions of our death. But within this realm of choicelessness, we do choose how we live.
>
> —Joseph Epstein

OVERVIEW OF THE HOLOCAUST

The Holocaust was the planned destruction of approximately 6 million Jews by the Nazis and their followers in Europe between 1933 and 1945. The German government, which was run by the National Socialist (Nazi) party, decided to annihilate all the Jews in Europe. The Nazis called their plan for Jewish annihilation the "final solution."

Five million Gypsies (also known as Roma), East Europeans, Communists, Jehovah's Witnesses, people with illnesses or disabilities, homosexuals, and political prisoners were also murdered by the Nazis during the Holocaust. Millions of other people were imprisoned and used for slave labor. These victims were professors, children, artists, business owners, grandparents, priests—people from all walks of life. They were killed because the Nazis, who were headed by German *führer* (leader) Adolf Hitler, thought that law, justice, and rules of decent human behavior did not apply to everyone. People who were different from them were considered to be threatening and inferior.

Adolf Hitler's Germany

Germany was part of the losing side in World War I (1914–1918) and was very poor economically afterward. The winning countries created the Treaty of Versailles, which forced Germany to pay war damages that amounted to billions of dollars. When the Great Depression of 1929 hit, the German people faced even more economic hardships. In this shaky condition, the German public welcomed Hitler.

Adolf Hitler did not possess the compassion, integrity, and wisdom that are the qualities of a truly great leader. What he did have was charisma, persuasiveness, and a desperate country that was vulnerable to his magnetism and looking for scapegoats. Hitler told the Germans they were superior people and that the Jews were responsible for Germany's problems. Although Germany was known for being an educated, cultured country, and a hundred thousand Jews had fought for Germany in World War I, most non-Jewish Germans did not stand by their fellow citizens.

Hitler became chancellor of Germany on January 30, 1933, through a democratic election. He then decided that democracy was no longer needed and expelled other political parties, imprisoned people who opposed him, held public book burnings, and ruled as a dictator. Hitler called his administration the Third Reich, meaning the third German empire, and he said it would last a thousand years. The First Reich that Hitler refers to was the Holy Roman Empire (962–1806), and the Second Reich was the Bismarck Empire that began in 1871 and ended with Germany's defeat in the first World War (1914–1918).

Hitler thought the most important thing about people was not who they were as individuals, but what religion they practiced or what skin color they possessed. He wanted to have German "Aryans" rule everybody else in the world. Although the word *Aryan* originally referred to a person who speaks an Indo-European language, Hitler and his Nazi regime used *Aryan* to mean a Caucasian Gentile. They idealized people who were tall, blond, and blue-eyed and demonized people who were not, in spite of the fact that Hitler himself was short and had dark hair and eyes. Hitler believed that Aryans were responsible for all of humanity's accomplishments. He wanted to rid the world of Jews because he thought they would bring down Aryans.

On September 15, 1935, Hitler published the Nuremberg Laws, which denied Jews their rights and citizenship. When a government promotes injustice and crime against a group, the situation is ripe for genocide. Genocide is the killing of a race of people. On November 8, 1938, a Jewish teenager named Herschel Grynszpan shot a German official in Paris. Grynszpan was distraught about his Polish parents' deportation. The Nazis saw this murder as the perfect excuse to persecute all the Jews in Germany. On November 9, 1938, the Nazis burned synagogues, broke into homes and stores, and beat Jews in the street. Because of the many windows smashed by rampaging Nazis, this incident was called *Kristallnacht* ("Night of Broken Glass"). Kristallnacht marked what many people consider to be the beginning of the Holocaust.

Germany also took over Austria in March 1938. Anti-Semitism, or prejudice against Jews, was strong in Austria, so Hitler's ideas were not met with much resistance there. In the years to come, more than 50 percent of the Nazi officers who worked in the death camps were Austrian.[1] Beginning in 1939 extending through 1940, Germany invaded Poland, Czechoslovakia, Denmark, Norway, France, Belgium, Luxembourg, and the Netherlands. Bulgaria, Romania, and Hungary became allied with the Nazis in 1940. Jews in these countries experienced similar dangers from Nazis that Jews in Germany were facing. For Jews who wanted to escape, there were fewer and fewer places to go.

The Concentration Camps

World War II began on September 1, 1939, when Germany invaded Poland, causing Great Britain and France to declare war on Germany. That same year Hitler ordered that people who were mentally or physically disabled be murdered. The Nazis created six death camps in Poland in 1940 and began deporting Polish Jews to them. These camps were Auschwitz, Treblinka, Sobibor, Chelmno, Majdanek, and

This map shows Europe in August 1940. By this time, the Germans had occupied Poland, Luxembourg, Denmark, Norway, France, Belgium, and the Netherlands.

Belzec. In the occupied countries the Nazis forced Jews into "ghettos," which were crowded, enclosed slums where hunger and disease ran rampant. From there, people were taken to concentration camps, where they were forced to do labor in horrible conditions or immediately killed. In the death camps Jews, along with Gypsies and others, were murdered in huge numbers in gas chambers.

When people reached the concentration camps, they would quickly be divided into groups of those who would die and those who would do forced labor, although the new arrivals were not told why they were being sent in different directions. Children, pregnant women, the elderly, and the sick were sent to the side that would be killed. Mothers often accompanied their children, although sometimes they were forced to separate. Family members might suspect but not be sure what had happened to their children, sisters, brothers, parents, aunts, uncles, cousins, and grandparents. Some people were chosen for medical experimentation, and they were kept alive so doctors such as Auschwitz's Dr. Josef Mengele could conduct painful, disfiguring, even deadly "scientific" experiments.

The Nazis used many inhuman methods to force Jews to their deaths. Sometimes the Nazis used shock and fear. They grabbed Jews out of their beds at night, threw them onto incredibly packed trains, shone bright lights in their faces as they stepped off, yelled at them, and hurried them to the gas chambers. Or the Nazis lied, promising to resettle them in a nicer place. The Nazis would even have choirs singing or orchestras playing when people got off the trains. They would tell the people who were chosen to die that they would have coffee and food after their "shower." But the only place they would go after their shower was to a crematorium, which was a large oven for burning bodies.

The Holocaust victims exhibited many forms of resistance, from physical combat to sustaining their faith and customs to simply refusing to give up even under the worst possible conditions. When World War II ended, approximately 11 million Jews and other civilians had perished. The Holocaust affected not only its survivors and their children, but also those who witnessed the death camps. The horrors of the Holocaust still touch us today.

1 Chapter

LIBERATION: A SURVIVOR'S VIEW

O n the day Alex Gross was liberated from the German concentration camp Buchenwald, he was sixteen years old, five feet nine and a half inches tall, and sixty pounds. It was April 1945, and he had been in concentration camps, on death marches, or in hiding for three years. Alex and others in the camps were expecting to be liberated because they heard the sounds of planes overhead and explosions nearby, but they had been bitterly disappointed before. They thought they would be freed in January when they were in Auschwitz, a concentration camp in Poland, but instead the Nazis had decided to move them.

Death Marches

Now that it looked as if the Allies would win the war, the Nazis wanted to destroy as much evidence of what they were doing as possible to prevent recrimination from the Allies. They also wanted to kill as many Jewish people as they could. They took sixty thousand people from Auschwitz on a three-day death march to Gleiwitz, another camp. The Jews were so weak from abuse and lack of food that out of the sixty thousand marchers, only eight thousand made it to Gleiwitz alive. From there, the survivors of the march were put on open-roofed, cattle-carrying railroad cars and transported to Buchenwald in the freezing cold. The train carrying Alex Gross contained 120 people; only eight of them survived the trip.[1]

Alex considered the conditions in Buchenwald to be better than those in Auschwitz. He was shocked to receive two slices of real bread; for a year he had only been given bread made of sawdust. Starvation, beatings, hard labor, and the strenuous trip weakened the survivors. When the liberators finally arrived at Buchenwald, Alex was not completely conscious. When Alex saw an American tank roll up and a soldier come out, he says he thought he was seeing one of God's angels.[2]

How Did Holocaust Survivors Feel at Liberation?

Holocaust survivors felt many conflicting emotions during the liberation of the concentration camps. Like Alex Gross, some felt relieved, happy, and eager to find any surviving family members. Having endured so much, however, many people were still afraid the Nazis would return. Josef Rosensaft, a survivor of the camp at Bergen-Belsen says, "We, the cowed and emaciated inmates of the camp, did not believe we were free. It seemed to us a dream which would soon turn again into cruel reality."[3]

Others were not sure what to do next because their families had been killed and they had no home to go to. Survivor Sonia Reznik Rosenfeld remembers a Russian officer telling the women he liberated, "You are free! Go where your hearts desire. Our Red Army has freed you from murderous hands." She describes the survivors' response:

> Everyone lay motionless, no one could utter a word. It is impossible to be freed when one already has one leg underground. As I could speak Russian better than anyone there, I told the officer that we were half-dead people, and I asked him where we would go, and how we would get there as none of us had a home any more for Hitler's hordes had shot everyone's family.[4]

Some people, both children and adults, were so hurt by their experiences under the Nazi government and by the deaths of their families that after liberation they committed suicide. They did not feel they had the strength to start over. Even though the Nazis did not kill these people directly, the responsibility for their deaths still lies with the Nazi actions.

Many survivors of the camps wanted to forget about the horrors they had endured and try to start new lives. Others realized that they could not forget what had happened. They wanted to spend their lives working to honor the victims, making sure the war criminals were brought to justice, and ensuring that in the future no other people would be the victims of genocide.

One such survivor was Helen Waterford. After the Russians liberated her from Kratzau (a work camp in Czechoslovakia), she began thinking about how important it was to give a firsthand account of the Holocaust. Eventually, she would travel throughout the United States, talking with people about the destructiveness of hate.

After his rescue Simon Wiesenthal decided to work with the American War Crimes Unit. He wanted to provide information about the Nazi war criminals out of respect for the dead, who could not seek their own justice. He also wanted to regain a sense that the world was humane and that civilized law could prevail over madness.[5]

Survivor Elie Wiesel educated people about the Holocaust by writing books about his experiences. In the powerful book *Night*, Wiesel writes,

> Never shall I forget that night, the first night in camp, which has turned my life into one long night, seven times cursed and seven times sealed. Never shall I forget that smoke. Never shall I forget the faces of the children, whose bodies I saw turned into wreaths of smoke beneath a silent blue sky.[6]

Night became a worldwide best-seller. Wiesel continues to write and lecture about the Holocaust. He won the Nobel Peace Prize in 1986.

It is difficult to imagine rounding up and murdering millions of unarmed strangers—babies, men, women, children, teenagers—because they were different. It is hard to imagine how afraid those people were when they were taken to the concentration camps, or how they felt as they were taken from their families, or when they saw their family members killed before their eyes.

How Did Liberators Respond to Concentration Camps?

The horror of the concentration camps was difficult for the Allied soldiers to face upon liberation. Even a general who had seen a lot of wartime activity was not prepared for the reality of the camps. General Dwight D. Eisenhower said:

> I have never felt able to describe my emotional reactions when I first came face to face with indisputable evidence of Nazi brutality and ruthless disregard of every shred of decency. Up to that time I had known about it only generally or through secondary sources. I am certain, however, that I have never at any other time experienced an equal sense of shock.[7]

Sergeant William Scott, one of the American soldiers who liberated Alex Gross and the other survivors at Buchenwald, said that he remembered thinking before they arrived at the concentration camp that "there is no place as horrible as we have been told."[8] After they arrived, however, he thought what they had been told was nothing in comparison to the reality of it. He saw "all forms of dismemberment of the human body . . . incinerators choked with human bones, dissected heads and bodies."[9] Displays of human body parts were placed on shelves by the doors of the barracks so that the prisoners would see them as they went in and out of the building. He asked himself how an educated country such as Germany could allow this type of

mass murder and psychotic behavior to take place, but he had no answers.[10]

American soldier Henry Allen said this about his experiences at the Mauthausen concentration camp in Austria:

> That is something you want to forget. . . . It was hard to concentrate on your everyday job because it could be me in that condition. It could have been my brother, my mother, my father, my sister. It could have been my family, but it so happened, I was an American from the land of the free. The memories are still there. You don't shake them entirely.[11]

Because of the rampant illness in the camps, the American soldiers were not always allowed inside, but those who were permitted in often found it to be a profoundly moving experience. Sergeant Abel Jack Schwartz, who also helped liberate Buchenwald, said, "I had witnessed many battlefield deaths. I considered myself to be tough, and inured to the sight and smell of death. However, at this sight, I just cried and cried."[12] In 1995 Lieutenant Charles Ferree, who saw five Nazi death camps, said, "After Dachau, I burned my uniform in a vain attempt to rid myself of the death smell. It's still with me, fifty years later."[13]

The Americans were so horrified by what they found that they would often bring local Germans from the surrounding areas through the concentration camps so they could witness the horror there. Buchenwald survivor Alex Gross heard one such German woman as she was being taken through the camp, shouting that the camps were just American propaganda. She said the Germans were too civilized and cultured to be a part of it. Gross recognized the woman from the previous month when he had been brought to her family farm and forced to work there. While Gross was working, this woman had witnessed her son whipping him with a stick. Rather than make her son stop, she told him that he was being too nice to the Jews. She brought out a pot of boiling water and poured it on Alex. He told an American soldier that he recognized the woman and also told him what she had done.[14]

Alex Gross recalled, "Most of us were more dead than alive, but the American soldiers really tried to nurse us back to life. It was beyond description how wonderful they were."[15] Tragically, however, when the soldiers gave survivors chocolate bars they had in their pockets—in an attempt to help the starving people—the chocolate often killed them. Many people died because their bodies could not handle having rich food after being without anything to eat for so long.

Where Did Holocaust Survivors Go?

Some of the concentration camps were turned into Displaced Persons (DP) Camps, which were initially run by the Allies and later by the United Nations Relief and Rehabilitation Administration. The war had turned millions of people into refugees. Lieutenant Charles Ferree said,

> Americans working to sort the people out told us stories of how difficult their job was. Many displaced people did not want to return to their homes. Jews didn't want to return to Poland, Gypsies had no safe place to go, Russians were afraid to return for fear of being put to death as traitors. Most expressed a desire to go to the [United] States or Palestine.[16]

Palestine was a British mandated territory in the Middle East between the Mediterranean Sea and the Jordan River. Today, Palestine is known as Israel and the West Bank. The British, who were in charge of granting visas to go to Palestine, only gave six thousand people visas. The United States also had strict limits on the number of visas that were granted.

The displaced Jews were rightfully concerned about returning to Poland. In July 1946, in the Polish town of Kielce, the Jews who had returned there had their weapons taken away by the police. The next day, they were attacked by a mob. Forty-two people were killed and many others were wounded. When word of this slaughter spread, one hundred thousand Jews in Poland fled the country in search of a safer home.[17] The tragedy of the Holocaust continued to affect eight hundred fifty thousand people who still had nowhere to go even two years after the war ended.

In many countries during the Holocaust, Jews' possessions were stolen while they were in the camps. This robbery made returning to their homes impossible. They were forced to start over with nothing. Only the people from Denmark acted as a group on behalf of their Jewish citizens. Danish Jews who survived the Holocaust were able to return to their homes and other possessions. They were among the lucky few whose fellow citizens had recognized their common humanity.

Between 1933 and 1945 Jewish culture and society took a tremendous blow. Seventy-two percent of the prewar Jewish population in Europe was murdered during those years. Although the Nazis tried to get rid of the evidence, their crimes were on such a large scale that "the Allies captured no fewer than 3,000 tons of documents and photographs relating to the camps."[18] This evidence would be used in the trials of war criminals. Although Adolf Hitler killed himself at the end of the war and many other Nazis eluded capture, in 1946 an International Military Tribunal tried twenty-two Nazi leaders for their war crimes in the famous Nuremberg Trials. Nineteen Nazi leaders would be convicted and three would be acquitted.

Chapter 2

VICTORY IN EUROPE

World War II began September 1, 1939, when Germany invaded Poland. Great Britain and France, who had agreed to defend Poland, declared war on Germany. The Axis powers (Germany, Italy, and Japan) fought the Allies (Great Britain, France, the Soviet Union, and the United States) throughout Europe, Africa, and Asia. The United States entered the war on December 7, 1941, after Japan bombed the United States's Pearl Harbor.

On June 6, 1944, United States general Dwight Eisenhower led the Allied invasion onto the beaches of Normandy, France. Over five thousand ships and eight thousand aircraft carrying more than one hundred fifty thousand American, Canadian, and British soldiers as well as weaponry and supplies stormed Normandy.[1] This invasion, known as D-day, proved to be vitally important to the war. D-day resulted in the Allies pushing the Axis front line back into Germany.

Many people in the German-occupied countries heard about D-day and became excited at the possibility of freedom. Teenager Anne Frank wrote from her attic hiding place in Holland, "Could we be granted victory this year, 1944? We don't know yet, but hope is revived within me; it gives us fresh courage, and makes us strong again."[2] Tragically, Anne Frank and her sister, Margot, died in the Bergen-Belsen concentration camp two months before the end of World War II.

On July 20, 1944, a group of German officers and others led by Count Claus von Stauffenberg attempted to assassinate Hitler with a time bomb. Although the conspirators believed the war was lost, they wanted to salvage Germany's dignity by having Germans be the ones to dispose of Hitler. They wanted to show the world that not all Germans supported Hitler, as well as to try to end the war on better terms with the Allies.[3] When the bomb exploded, several members of his staff were killed, but Hitler escaped with only a wounded arm and punctured eardrum. At least two thousand people were accused of conspiring in the assassination plot and were sentenced to death.[4] Many had no involvement with the plot. This was not Count von Stauffenberg's first plan to assassinate Hitler, but it was his last.

The Allies Push Forward

Russian troops were advancing on the German east and north sides, while the other Allied forces made headway from the west. The Russian Army found the abandoned remains of the Majdanek death camp in Poland on July 24, 1944. The soldiers did not find the horrors that would await Allied troops in the camps that still contained prisoners, but they did find haunting reminders of what had happened there. Near the camp was a warehouse "bursting with 800,000 shoes that had once belonged to Nazi victims."[5] Hitler was angry with his SS troops (the elite Nazi division in charge of the concentration camps) because they had not destroyed all the evidence before the Soviets arrived.[6]

On August 1, 1944, when the citizens of Warsaw, Poland, heard that the Soviets were approaching, they spurred to action against the German soldiers in their city. The Polish Home Army expected to receive help from the Soviet troops and attacked the Nazis, but Joseph Stalin, the Communist Russian leader, refused to lend them any assistance. He thought the Polish Army was composed of anti-Communists, so he wanted the Poles and the Germans to kill each other. After two months of fighting, the Nazis crushed the Warsaw uprising.[7]

On the western front the American-led Allied troops kept driving back the German Army during the rest of 1944, until snowfall in December slowed their efforts. At this point the Germans decided to attack. In this battle, known as "The Battle of the Bulge," the Germans made progress at first, creating a "bulge" in the Allied front lines. Yet the Allies rallied quickly and forced them to retreat again.

The Nazi Reaction to Allied Success

Meanwhile the Nazis decided to evacuate Auschwitz. Realizing they were losing the war against the Allies, they still tried to win their war against unarmed Jews, Gypsies, and other minority groups. The Nazis also attempted to cover their tracks so the Allies would not know how many civilians they had killed. Alex Gross was taken on one of the death marches that the Nazis organized in their desperate attempt to empty the concentration camps and kill the remaining prisoners. Although the end of the war (and liberation) was near, victims of the camps endured severe hardships. "When it came, liberation was a slaughterhouse," said French survivor Robert Deneri.[8]

Ironically the German soldiers were seriously concerned about how they would be treated if they became prisoners at the mercy of the Soviets. Hitler's invasion of the Soviet Union earlier in the war had made the Soviets especially angry. When German troops surrendered, they tried to surrender to Americans. In an effort to make themselves look better to the Allies, the Nazis would occasionally give their prisoners food immediately before releasing them, telling the prisoners not to remember them as being too bad. Lithuanian survivor Dr. Edith Kramer-Freund said that "the SS wished us 'All the best' as they left the train at the Swiss frontier. . . . They knew that the end was coming and they wanted to make a good impression on the Swiss, and leave us with a good impression of them, to mitigate any

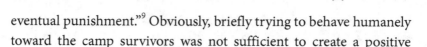

eventual punishment."[9] Obviously, briefly trying to behave humanely toward the camp survivors was not sufficient to create a positive impression.

The Allies' Future Plans

In February 1945 American president Franklin D. Roosevelt, British prime minister Winston Churchill, and Soviet premier Joseph Stalin met in Yalta, in the southern Soviet Union, for the Yalta Conference. During this meeting the leaders of the Allied nations made plans for the future after the war. They agreed to divide Germany into four zones that would each be governed by one of the Allies. They decided that Germany should pay for war damages and should not be allowed to develop a stronghold of weapons in the future. The leaders also thought that the Nazi commanders should be tried for their war crimes.

Meanwhile, the Allies fought to reach the Rhine River and enter Germany. On March 23, 1945, they were successful, and began a major crossing of the Rhine. During this month Anne Frank, the girl whose diary showed so many readers what life was like in hiding from the Nazis, died of typhus in Germany's Bergen-Belsen concentration camp.

Liberation of the Concentration Camps

As the Allies came through Germany and Poland, they liberated the concentration camps. It was a shocking experience for the Allied troops. The soldiers could not believe that civilized human beings could behave so savagely. Many soldiers wanted to know how much the German civilians knew and how they could let it happen.

The troops were not the only witnesses to the atrocities; camp victims who were still alive needed serious medical care. Nurses and doctors also saw what the prisoners had endured. For instance, American nurses in two army hospitals cared for people who had been in Dachau. The nurses saw that the inmates had been starved and tortured; they had gangrene, frozen feet, tuberculosis, and typhus. Even with intensive care, thousands of people died after liberation.[10]

Survivor Shalom Cholawshi described his liberation as being great joy mixed with incredible sadness. He says, "If only they had come two years earlier! Now that the day of liberation was here, there was no one left to free."[11]

On April 5, 1945, a sub-camp of the German concentration camp at Buchenwald was accidentally discovered as Allies searched for a "secret Nazi communications center."[12] This was the first inhabited camp to be discovered by British or American troops. General Eisenhower was deeply shocked by what he saw at the camp. Although logistically it was not possible for all the American soldiers to see the camps, General Eisenhower thought every American soldier who was not fighting on the front line should come see "what he is fighting against."[13]

The Nordhausen-Dora labor camps were discovered on April 11, 1945. The Allies found three thousand corpses and seven hundred people barely alive. The Allies had German civilians help dig graves. Some Allied soldiers said that so much work needed to be done in the camps (between attempting to save the living and burying the dead) that soldiers had to focus on the task at hand, or the horror of the situation would overwhelm them.[14]

Journalists and photographers also visited the concentration camps. In her autobiography, photographer Margaret Bourke-White says, "People often ask me how it is possible to photograph such atrocities. I have to work with a veil over my mind. In photographing the murder camps, the protective veil was so tightly drawn that I hardly knew what I had taken until I saw prints of my own photographs."[15]

Dachau Discovered

Adolf Hitler's first concentration camp, Dachau, was liberated on April 29, 1945, by American soldiers. The Americans had expected

Nazi retaliation when they arrived, but instead they found skeletal captives—survivors—who greeted them waving an American flag they had made themselves. In a short time, the liberators experienced a wide range of emotions. They felt horror and rage at the conditions of the prisoners, and they saw the prisoners' joy, tears, and desire for revenge. In their fury some American soldiers killed German guards who had remained in Dachau and also allowed some prisoners to kill guards.

Allies who were witnesses at Dachau published a report containing a history, diary, and description of the concentration camp, as well as personal testimonies. The liberators asked the German people in the nearby town of Dachau how they could let this evil go on. The Dachau townspeople confessed they were too scared to get involved. In their report, the Allies said that there was a "fearsome shadow" hanging over everyone "in a state in which crime ha(d) been incorporated and called the government."[16] However, even though the government made it difficult for people to make moral choices without being afraid of what would happen, some people did. In any situation, even one as bleak as Nazi Germany, there is always a moral choice to be made.

Outside the Camps

The Allies also discovered horrors in places other than the concentration camps. In Ousterburg, Germany, they found a barn in which SS troops had burned their prisoners. The SS troops had forced the people into the barn, set fire to it, and then stood outside with machine guns to make sure no one escaped. People tried to dig their way out from the sides of the barn, but were immediately shot: "When American troops came on the scene, the first thing they noticed were the heads of these dead prisoners peering from underneath the wall."[17]

As the Allies pushed forward, they met groups of people roaming the countryside. The people—refugees, survivors trying to find their families, and others in need of help—had been hiding from the

Nazis and were finally able to leave their hiding places as the Allies liberated Europe.

Hiding in one Belgian convent at the end of the war were ten Jewish adults, twenty-eight Jewish children, plus Allied parachutists and resistance fighters. The convent's Mother Superior was given a medal for her bravery.[18] Children all over Europe who had been separated from their parents waited eagerly for their parents to return, afraid that they did not survive. Some children were too young to even remember their parents from before the war.

As the Allies had more successes in Germany, Adolf Hitler realized that his dreams of world domination and killing the entire Jewish race were over. He eluded capture by killing himself on April 30, 1945. Germany surrendered to the Allied powers on May 7, 1945, which is known as V-E day for "Victory in Europe."

The Allies were still fighting the Axis power Japan on the Pacific front, but the battle with the Third Reich had finally ended.

TRIALS OF MAJOR NAZI LEADERS AT NUREMBERG

O n November 14, 1945, in Nuremberg, Germany, the Allies began the trials of twenty-two Nazi leaders for their war crimes. The Third Reich had come full circle. In the 1930s, Nuremberg had been the site of enthusiastic annual Nazi party rallies where Hitler spread his anti-Semitic propaganda. The 1935 laws that took away Jewish citizenship and rights were also named after Nuremberg. Now some of the men who were responsible for taking part in Hitler's regime were facing their actions in that very town.

British major Airey Neave was twenty-nine when he was assigned to work for the Allies at the Nuremberg Trials. He felt inexperienced compared to the judges and lawyers at the trials, but like many young people of his generation, he had been through years of hardship. Neave had been captured by the Germans as a prisoner of war and had escaped more than once. He had seen life under Nazi rule firsthand, and it made him fiercely angry. He says, "In the court-room, I could feel the presence of dead millions. They were there throughout the trial, sad phantoms from the gas chamber come as witnesses to Nuremberg."[1] In spite of his anger toward the Nazis, Neave believed strongly in that the defendants should be tried fairly.

In the Allied countries diverse opinions arose about trying the Nazi leaders for their war crimes. Everyone from world leaders to soldiers to private citizens reacted to the trials. Some people, including British prime minister Winston Churchill, believed it would be better to kill the Nazi war criminals without a trial as the Allied troops came into Germany.[2] They thought that since the Nazis had not behaved fairly to their victims, the Nazis did not deserve the benefit of a trial. Other people held the view that it would not be fair for the defeated Nazis to be tried by their conquerors. They believed the Germans themselves should try the Nazis. Still other people hated the Soviet Union so much that they did not want to be part of trials that included Russians as judges.

The Necessity of the Nuremberg Trials

Others believed, for a variety of reasons, it was necessary for an international court to try the Nazis for their crimes. First, they thought this was an opportunity to illustrate that the world was not going to allow war crimes to go unpunished, and that a new standard for international justice was being established. Robert Jackson, an American Supreme Court Justice who served as one of the prosecutors at Nuremberg, said in his opening speech: "The wrongs which we seek to condemn and punish have been so calculated, so malignant, and so devastating, that civilization cannot tolerate their being ignored, because it cannot survive their being repeated."[3]

Second, many people felt it was important to show that the countries who favored justice and law had won the war. During the Third Reich, justice had been tossed aside in favor of corruption and absolute power for the few, and fear and lack of human rights for the many. The trials were an opportunity to establish the return of civilized law.

Third, after World War I, the Allies had asked Germany to try 901 of its war criminals (and provided incriminating evidence). Germany acquitted 888 of them, and the other thirteen (who were given brief sentences) were considered to be war heroes.[4] A repeat of these trials would have been a bitter pill to swallow for the concentration camp survivors.

Rules of War

During the Nuremberg Trials, Nazis were to be tried for violating the international rules of war and other crimes. Although war seems by its nature not to be controlled, rules do exist that govern behaviors during war toward civilians, prisoners of war, and neutral countries as well as behavior during a truce or cease-fire. People have found that these guidelines are necessary because they limit the destructiveness of war and make peace possible afterward.

Acceptable behavior during wartime has changed throughout history. In the 1800s and 1900s certain common rules were agreed upon by most nations, including Germany. In 1907 at The Hague, Netherlands, an important international conference took place at which many war regulations were adopted. These included rules for the humane treatment of prisoners of war and policies regarding the property and belongings of the defeated. Private property was not to be stolen by the victors. This rule was broken by the Nazis on a huge scale during World War II.

The Charges

Various defendants at the Nuremberg Trials were charged with up to four different crimes. Almost all were accused of committing war crimes. War crimes are defined as violations of international agreements about how the military should behave during wars, such as the mistreatment of prisoners, murder, or forced labor of occupied civilian populations.

Most defendants were also charged with committing crimes against humanity, which included murder, deportation, and religious persecution. All were charged with conspiracy, being involved in "a common plan to commit a crime in the future."[5] Some were also charged with crimes against peace, which include the "planning, preparing, initiating, or waging of a war of aggression."[6]

The Defendants

Adolf Hitler, the commander of the Nazi regime, was not available to be tried for his war crimes, nor was Joseph Goebbels, his minister of Propaganda, because they both committed suicide when they realized Germany had lost the war. However, the man who organized both the Gestapo and concentration camps (Hermann Goering), the Nazi governor general of Poland (Hans Frank), the chief of the Reich Security Main Office (Ernst Kaltenbrunner), and nineteen other Nazi leaders were tried. Each of the defendants were allowed to choose the attorney who would defend him in court.

The Judges

Eight judges sat on the Nuremberg Trials' International Military Tribunal—two each from France, Great Britain, the United States, and the Soviet Union. The head judge was Great Britain's Lord Justice Lawrence, who asked the people involved in the trials to take their duties seriously and behave according to the "sacred principles of law and justice."[7] Although the extreme military and political tension that would become the Cold War was already starting between the Soviet Union and countries in the West, they were able to work cooperatively throughout the trials.

All defendants pleaded "not guilty" to the accusations. Almost all claimed they were just following orders and that Hitler was the one responsible (Goering accepted responsibility for the orders he gave, but defended the actions of the Third Reich as being what the Nazis thought would help the German people).[8] These trials were historic events. The International Military Tribunal judges concluded that people have responsibility for their own choices and actions, regardless of whether someone else had commanded them to carry out these orders. Journalist Victor Bernstein says the judgment at the Nuremberg Trials showed,

> It is no longer an excuse for a criminal that he has killed not one man, nor two, but millions. It is no longer the warmaker's privilege that his sole judge shall be the historian who, coming upon the scene ten, twenty, fifty years too late, can but beat a dead dog. From now on the warmaker can be punished today, like any other common murderer.[9]

Many defendants also tried to say they did not know that the war crimes were taking place, but the prosecution was able to show evidence that they did. For instance, Hans Frank denied knowing anything about the Polish concentration camps until the prosecution brought in his thirty-six volume journal as evidence, which proved that he did.[10] American prosecutor Robert Jackson said, in response to the claim that the defendants did not know what Hitler's plans were, "The plans of Adolf Hitler for aggression were just as secret as *Mein Kampf* [Hitler's political manifesto], of which over six million copies were published in Germany."[11] Scholar Eugene Davidson says, "The crimes of the Nazi leadership were in fact indisputable; the record was so overwhelming that the prosecution found its chief difficulty to be mastering the tons of documents that came to Nuremberg in truckloads."[12]

Evidence from the Nuremberg Trials exposed the Nazi plan to eliminate the Jewish people and other groups they thought were inferior and revealed the horrifying slave labor program. Publicly uncovering the truth about the Holocaust can be considered one of the most important outcomes of the Nuremberg Trials.

Another result of the trials was that they showed that the Nazi leaders were not impressive figures. Because they had powerfully committed such atrocities, people expected them to look evil. The Nazis, however, looked ordinary, sometimes even pathetic or ridiculous, and hardly capable of the crimes they had committed. Victor Bernstein, who was present at the trials, says, "Meet Jodl, Keitel, Doenitz, Rosenberg, Frank, Speer, Fritzsche under other circumstances, and you might be meeting a salesman, a physician, a lawyer,

The Nuremberg Trials' Verdicts

Defendant	Conspiracy	Crimes Against Peace	War Crimes	Crimes Against Humanity	Sentence
Hermann Goering	Guilty	Guilty	Guilty	Guilty	Death by hanging
Rudolph Hess	Guilty	Guilty	Not Guilty	Not Guilty	Life imprisonment
Joachim von Ribbentrop	Guilty	Guilty	Guilty	Guilty	Death by hanging
Wilhelm Keitel	Guilty	Guilty	Guilty	Guilty	Death by hanging
Ernst Kaltenbrunner	Not Guilty	———	Guilty	Guilty	Death by hanging
Alfred Rosenberg	Guilty	Guilty	Guilty	Guilty	Death by hanging
Hans Frank	Not Guilty	———	Guilty	Guilty	Death by hanging
Wilhelm Frick	Not Guilty	Guilty	Guilty	Guilty	Death by hanging
Julius Streicher	Not Guilty	———	———	Guilty	Death by hanging
Walter Funk	Not Guilty	Guilty	Guilty	Guilty	Life imprisonment
Hjalmar Schacht	Not Guilty	Not Guilty	———	———	Acquitted
Karl Doenitz	Not Guilty	Guilty	Guilty	———	10 years imprisonment
Erich Raeder	Guilty	Guilty	Guilty	———	Life imprisonment
Baldur von Schirach	Not Guilty	———	———	Guilty	20 years imprisonment
Fritz Sauckel	Not Guilty	Not Guilty	Guilty	Guilty	Death by hanging
Alfred Jodl	Guilty	Guilty	Guilty	Guilty	Death by hanging
Martin Bormann (in absentia)	Not Guilty	———	Guilty	Guilty	Death by hanging
Franz von Papen	Not Guilty	Not Guilty	———	———	Acquitted
Arthur Seyss-Inquart	Not Guilty	Guilty	Guilty	Guilty	Death by hanging
Albert Speer	Not Guilty	Not Guilty	Guilty	Guilty	20 years imprisonment
Constantin von Neurath	Guilty	Guilty	Guilty	Guilty	15 years imprisonment
Hans Fritzsche	Not Guilty	———	Not Guilty	Not Guilty	Acquitted

a real estate broker."[13] Although people might have been disappointed that the Nazis' physical appearance did not live up to their
reputation, there was a lesson in it—it is impossible to tell what
someone is capable of by looking at his or her appearance. This is
true of greatness as well as evil.

The trials lasted a little over ten months, and in the end, nineteen
men were found guilty and three were acquitted. Twelve of the men
who were found guilty were sentenced to death by hanging, and the
other seven were given prison sentences ranging from ten years to
life. Many people were surprised that not all the men were found
guilty and sentenced to death. However, those who had said that the
Allies had tried to create fair trials pointed to the verdicts as proof
that they had convicted the defendants according to the evidence,
not out of spite.

Although tens of thousands of people had committed war crimes
by "initiating, planning, and directing the killing operations," and
hundreds of thousands more were directly involved in the persecution and murder of innocent civilians, the famous Nuremberg Trials
of 1945 were only for the Nazi leaders.[14] Twelve more trials of Nazis
by the Allies took place from 1946 to 1949 in which 185 defendants
were tried. About half were found guilty. Many war criminals
escaped prosecution because the Cold War between the Soviet Union
and the United States distracted the two superpowers from pursuing
them.

The trials at Nuremberg were expected to usher in a new era of
justice and peace. Since then, however, many new war crimes have
been committed worldwide, such as the nearly 2 million Cambodians
who were murdered by the Khmer Rouge regime in the 1970s.
Genocide has not been stopped. In 1995 Jutta Limbaugh, president
of Germany's highest court, stated that the legacy of the Nuremberg
Trials has not been that they stopped war crimes but that they placed
responsibility for such crimes at the feet of the people who commit
them.

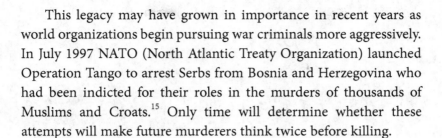

This legacy may have grown in importance in recent years as world organizations begin pursuing war criminals more aggressively. In July 1997 NATO (North Atlantic Treaty Organization) launched Operation Tango to arrest Serbs from Bosnia and Herzegovina who had been indicted for their roles in the murders of thousands of Muslims and Croats.[15] Only time will determine whether these attempts will make future murderers think twice before killing.

FINDING A HOME: THE CREATION OF ISRAEL

P oet Robert Frost said, "Home is the place where, when you go there, they have to take you in."[1] After the Holocaust, many Jewish survivors felt they had no home. Returning to their Eastern European countries seemed bleak (their families and possessions were gone) and dangerous (anti-Semitism still remained). Making a new home in another country was an option for only a fraction of the refugees, because many countries would only allow them to enter in small numbers.

Zion

To many displaced persons, going to Palestine seemed like a natural idea. Palestine, a small country in the Middle East, is considered holy by the believers of three religions: Christianity, Islam, and Judaism. Christians believe Palestine is the birthplace of Jesus; Muslims believe Muhammad, Islam's founder, ascended to heaven from Jerusalem (a city in Palestine).

Jewish people thought of Palestine, which they referred to as Zion, as a holy place because it was the birthplace of Judaism. They lived there for over a thousand years until Roman armies invaded, causing many Jews to flee. The idea that Jews would return to Zion became part of their religious rituals. Some Jews felt it was necessary for them to be in Zion for the messiah to arrive and the "Day of Redemption" to occur.

During the 1800s most of the Jews in the world were living in Eastern Europe, particularly in Russia. Before 1855 Russian Jews were treated by their fellow Russians according to the "medieval stereotype," that they were greedy Christ killers.[2] Judaism existed before Christianity and was the first monotheistic religion (religion based on a belief in only one deity). Christianity is similar to Judaism, but Christianity centers on the premise that Jesus Christ was the son of God. Judaism, although it does acknowledge that Jesus Christ existed, does not hold that Christ was the son of God. This difference has been a substantial source of Christian hostility toward Jews.[3]

There was a period of "enlightenment" in Russia after Alexander II became the new tsar in 1855, and the Jews were treated better by their fellow citizens. This was, however, a brief era of peace for the Jews. In 1881 Alexander III had Alexander II assassinated and took over the throne. Alexander III wanted his country to be homogeneous (made up of only one kind of people), so he issued anti-Jewish laws and encouraged a series of pogroms (planned persecutions) of Jews. Alexander III said he wanted to kill Jews, force some to leave, and have the rest give up their Jewish religion and culture. Two and a half million Jews did leave Russia. At this time Russian Zionist Leo Pinsker wrote that Jews needed a homeland because they could not count on other countries to treat them fairly.[4]

Jews in the West had been treated better than the Eastern Jews, which was why the "Dreyfus Affair" in France came as such a surprise. In Paris in 1894 Captain Alfred Dreyfus (a Jewish man) was tried for treason, but during the trial it appeared that he was really being tried because he was a Jew. Paris was known for being more intellectual and progressive than other cities, which is why Jews in Western Europe were shocked by the trial. Captain Dreyfus was found guilty and sent to Devil's Island. Theodor Herzl, an Austrian-

Jewish journalist who witnessed the trial, was so affected that he began writing about the need for a separate Jewish state.[5] Herzl went on to found the Zionist Organization in 1897 at the first Zionist Congress.

The Need for a Homeland

There are two different kinds of "Zionism" (which means the desire for a Jewish National Home in Zion)—religious Zionism and political Zionism. Religious Zionism encourages its followers to live in Zion because it is the Holy Land and so that the "Day of Redemption" can occur. Political Zionism is driven by the belief that Jews need their own country because other countries do not reliably accord them all the rights of citizenship. Historically, political Zionism was considered less necessary when Jews felt well accepted in other countries. Consequently, its popularity increased with threats to their well-being.

From 1882 to 1939 thousands of Jews made "aliyahs" to Palestine. *Aliyah* means "going up" and is how Jews refer to immigrating to Palestine. These immigrants made a Jewish state possible by changing the makeup of the country's population.

Palestine was under Turkish control at the beginning of World War I, as it had been for four hundred years. Turkey joined Germany to fight against the Allies, and after the war, the League of Nations (the predecessor to the United Nations) mandated that Great Britain administer Palestine while preparing it for self-rule. In November 1917 the British foreign secretary Lord Arthur Balfour made the Balfour Declaration:

> His Majesty's Government view with favour the establishment in Palestine of a national home for the Jewish people, and will use their best endeavors to facilitate the achievement of this object, it being clearly understood that nothing shall be done which may prejudice the civil and religious rights of existing non-Jewish communities in Palestine, or the rights and political status enjoyed by Jews in any other country.[6]

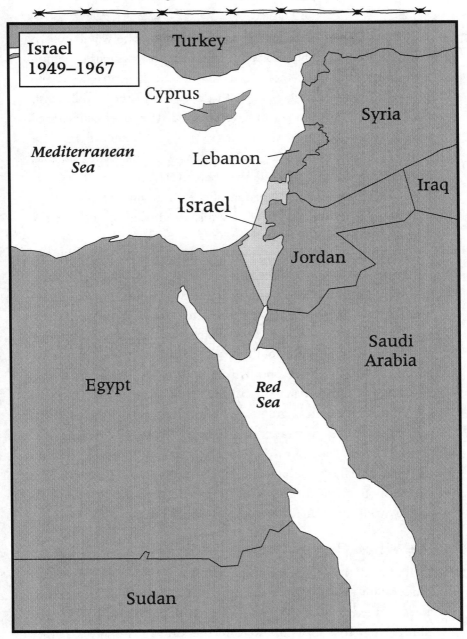

Israel
1949–1967

Turkey

Cyprus

Syria

Mediterranean Sea

Lebanon

Iraq

Israel

Jordan

Saudi Arabia

Egypt

Red Sea

Sudan

The Holocaust survivors did not find a peaceful refuge in Israel. The country has been plagued with war and violence throughout its existence.

However, British feelings on the question of who would govern Palestine seemed to be uncertain. Some support existed for letting Jews have their national home in Palestine, but the British also were concerned with keeping peace with the Arabs in the Middle East. Because the Arabs wanted to have an Arab state in Palestine, they were very much against the creation of a Jewish state there. The British wanted to maintain good relations with the Arab countries for political reasons and to have access to Arab oil. In 1922 Great Britain gave a substantial portion of the Palestinian territory they were governing to the Arabs. Today this area makes up the country of Jordan and the West Bank territory.[7]

Jewish immigration to Palestine increased in the 1930s due to the Third Reich and its effects on the European Jews. Henrietta Szold, an American who was worried about the health and conditions of the Jewish refugees in Palestine, raised money on their behalf. In 1932, in the face of worsening economic conditions and growing anti-Semitism, Szold realized a Holocaust was coming in Europe. She founded a "Youth Aliyah" to save Jewish children. The Youth Aliyah is said to have rescued fifty thousand children.

With the new immigrants, Jews laid the foundation for their national home. They created their own governing body called the Jewish Agency. They formed an unofficial military force, called the Haganah, which later became the national army. They also continued the tradition of "kibbutzim," which refers to farms run by groups of people living communally rather than by one family.

The White Paper

The persecution of Jews in Europe resulted in a sharp rise in Jewish immigration to Palestine in the mid-1930s. The Palestinian Arabs rioted in the late 1930s in response to the high numbers of Jewish immigrants. Great Britain, aware of the strategic impact that the Arabs could have once World War II began, issued a decree in 1937 that horrified the Jews. This decree, known as the White Paper, stated that only a limited number of Jews (about ten thousand per year) could immigrate to Palestine for the next five years, and after that, no more could come without Arab permission. It also stated that Great Britain would only allow a limited expanse of Palestinian land to be purchased by Jews. In addition, British prime minister Neville Chamberlain announced that "Britain would not let Palestine become a Jewish state."[8]

Jews were mortified by this decision, particularly in view of the plight of Jews in Europe, who desperately needed a place to go. They had expected the British to live up to the Balfour Declaration, which stated the British would help the Jews create their national home. Some still believed that they could change Great Britain's mind about the White Paper. Others gave up hope of British help at all. Regardless, the Jews wanted to join the fight against Germany, so Palestinian Jews found themselves fighting on the same side as the Allies even though they did not want to ally themselves with the British.

The Jewish Agency encouraged Jews to bring immigrants into the country despite the White Paper. There were some organized groups who had some successes, but often boats of immigrants were caught by the British and sent back to Europe or sent to a detention camp on the island of Cyprus. The refugees were once again caught up in the political maneuvering of many countries, and as a result, their lives were in danger.

In December 1941 the SS *Struma*, an old ship loaded with Jewish refugees, had to dock in Istanbul, Turkey, because it was in such bad shape that it could not finish the voyage to Palestine. Everyone on board needed to get off so the ship could be repaired, but the Turks would not let the refugees off the ship. They feared that if they let the refugees set foot in Turkey, they would stay, knowing they would be denied entry into Palestine. Great Britain was asked to allow the refugees into Palestine. If Great Britain agreed, the Turks would be willing to fix the ship. The British refused. The ship was forced to go back to sea, and it sank, killing 767 people, including 70 children.[9]

Toward the end of World War II, when cooperation with Great Britain did not seem as essential to the war cause, some Palestinian Jews began resisting the British presence in Palestine even more. Groups stole ammunition from the British to increase their supplies. Other extremist groups tried to use terrorist tactics to force the British to leave Palestine. The Arabs wanted to expel the British as well, but at the same time, they tried to prevent the creation of a Jewish state.

At war's end, at least one hundred thousand displaced persons wished to immigrate to Palestine. American opinion at the end of the war was in sympathy with the plight of the survivors, and President Harry Truman announced that the United States government supported letting all of them into Palestine immediately.[10] Great Britain wanted the United States to help govern Palestine, but the United States was reluctant to do so because they did not want to be committed to such a costly, contentious undertaking.[11]

Over the next year Palestine was in a state of extreme tension. While most of the British and the Jews in Palestine maintained a strained but nonviolent relationship, people on both sides used violent tactics. Jews living on the coast of Palestine saw ships carrying Holocaust survivors being turned away in large numbers. The Arabs worried about what would happen next. The British were uncertain about what to do.

The sight of Holocaust survivors on ships being turned away by British troops became a public relations nightmare for Great Britain. For instance, the refugees on the ship *Beauharnais* strung a banner across the deck that read "We survived Hitler. Death is no stranger to us. Nothing can keep us from our Jewish homeland. The blood be on your head if you fire on this unarmed ship."[12] People in the United States and Great Britain saw photographs of this incident and were sympathetic to the plight of the refugees.

In February 1947 Great Britain held the London Conference to attempt to resolve the problem in Palestine. The complicated London Conference plan suggested that a unitary state be created (one that was neither solely Jewish or Arabic).[13] When the ideas that came out of the conference were refused by both Jews and Arabs, Great Britain decided to turn over the Palestine question to the United Nations. The United Nations created a UN Special Committee on Palestine, which traveled to Palestine in May and gave its recommendations in August. On November 29, 1947, the United Nations voted to partition (divide) Palestine into Jewish and Arab states by 1949. The Jews rejoiced, but the Arabs were angry.

Although they were not supposed to do anything to obstruct the United Nations' decision to partition Palestine, the British leaders in Palestine made things difficult. In February 1948 Great Britain closed their government offices and courts, burned government files, shut down the oil refineries, let prisoners out of jails, and closed post offices.[14] A United Nations Commission was chosen to take over the government as the British closed their offices, but Great Britain did not allow the commission to enter Palestine until two weeks before they left.[15]

The Jews and the Arabs sensed a war brewing between them after the British left. Both groups had made steady preparations for battle during the months between the United Nations vote and the British expulsion from Palestine. Golda Meir (a member of the Histadrut Jewish labor organization who would later become prime minister of Israel) secretly went to see King Abdullah of Jordan to try to prevent the two countries from going to war, but she was unsuccessful.[16]

On May 14, 1948, British forces left Palestine. In the afternoon, the Jews proclaimed their Declaration of Independence, making Israel a Jewish nation-state. The next day the surrounding Arab countries of Lebanon, Syria, Iraq, Jordan, Saudi Arabia, and Egypt invaded Israel. They expected to be able to rapidly put an end to the new nation-state, but the fighting continued for more than a year. The better-organized Israeli Army was not only able to drive back the Arabs, but to capture additional territory.

Young survivors stand behind a barbed wire fence in Buchenwald concentration camp.

Although Jews and Arabs were able to live peacefully together for hundreds of years in the past, the desire of both groups to be self-governing in Palestine/ Israel and their lack of trust in each other has stood in the way of compromise for most of this century.

Chapter 5

SURVIVORS STARTING OVER

Most of the concentration camp survivors were young people, since almost all people over forty and under sixteen had been taken directly to the gas chambers or worked to death. The survivors resented the fact that the Nazis had taken away years of their youth and were eager to get on with living. Many survivors wanted to start a family right away to try to recreate the family they had lost.

They also wanted to continue with their education or with their careers. Vital years of their education had been lost, and survivors did not always have a chance to start again. Says Alex Gross, "There was not even a question about my continuing my education. I did not want to be a burden. I wanted to support myself."[1]

The children and adults who survived the Holocaust had led all kinds of lives in many different countries before the start of World War II. They had been professionals, laborers, students, and everything in between. Experiences during the Holocaust were varied too. They ranged from:

- the resistance fighter who spends years doing hard labor
- the twin who is the subject of medical experimentation
- the man in hiding who smothers his crying baby rather than have it risk the lives of the others
- the teenager whose job is loading dead bodies onto a truck
- the Jewish child who pretends to be Catholic and lives in a convent
- the member of the Polish underground who sneaks in and out of Auschwitz bringing news and goods

The experiences of the survivors after the war reflected how different their lives had been previously. What they had in common, though, was that they were people who had suffered, people who now had to "find a way of coming to terms with the wound it left."[2]

The Search for Loved Ones

After liberation many Holocaust survivors were in for a shock. They were happy that Germany's Third Reich was over, but they still had many problems to face. Survivor Alex Gross explains, "It is very difficult to suddenly find yourself without parents, without loved ones, to have to go out in the world. You come to a strange place; you don't know the language; you don't know the habits, the likes and dislikes; you don't know the people; and suddenly you've got to fit in and you've got to go to work."[3]

Life under the Nazis had been totally different from their lives before the Holocaust, and now they had to adjust to a new way of life. Children and teenagers who lived through the Holocaust had endured an identity-crushing experience just as they were trying to figure out who they were.[4] Most children had seen that their parents could not protect them the way they had expected them to, and their sense of security and trust, in both their parents and people in general, was damaged. Their sense of belonging and community had been turned upside down too, and now they had to find the strength to start over.

Many children were orphaned, and many others did not really know their parents because they had been separated during the war. When Alex Gross and two of his brothers were liberated from Buchenwald, the first thing they did was take a truck to Czechoslovakia to discover what had happened to the rest of their family. They came from a large family—seven children, parents, grandparents, aunts, uncles, and over forty cousins. They found one more brother in a refugee-gathering place in Prague, and he told them another brother was still alive.

Their sister arrived in Prague after being liberated from the Bergen-Belsen concentration camp. She brought the sad news that she thought their mother had been killed. Over time they discovered that, although their brothers and sister had survived the war, almost all of their other family members, including their forty cousins, had been murdered. They still kept hoping their parents would return. "You don't give up hope that easy," Alex says.[5]

One problem for many of the survivors was that they were not certain about what had happened to their loved ones. Even when they were positive their family and friends were dead, they usually did not have a place to go mourn them because most of the murder victims were cremated or buried in mass graves. For many people, the fact that their loved ones had not been buried or mourned properly made it difficult for them to accept their deaths.

After arriving in Czechoslovakia, Alex became ill again. As he lay in the hospital, he heard the doctors say they did not want to waste penicillin on him because he was not going to recover. He tore up a sheet to make a rope and lowered himself out the window to run away. Even though the doctors had thought Alex would not get better, he did, and he decided to go to England with his sister. At this time many orphans were being taken to English orphanages. Alex was still very upset about the deaths of his family and friends, and he was scared about not knowing English or the culture, but he says that being in England helped him. "People were so nice to me

in England that it started to give me faith in good people again," he says.[6]

The reaction of other people to the survivors could affect the survivors' outlook on life in a number of ways. Some people were very disappointed to find that they were treated as "living evidence of an event most people preferred to forget."[7] Others found that their old neighbors treated them as if the war had been their fault. When survivors returned to their homes in Eastern Europe, they often found that someone else was living there and that their possessions were gone. Czechoslovakian Franci Solar, for instance, returned to her home to find that many of her family's belongings had been taken by "friends" who did not expect her family to return. They refused to give back her family's possessions.

Dr. Edith Kramer-Freund, a survivor from Lithuania, received emotional and professional support from her friends, Ninon and Hermann Hesse. (Hermann Hesse, a German novelist and poet, won the 1946 Nobel Prize for literature.) She says, "Through Ninon, I gathered new hope."[8] Support and caring were, as you would expect, more helpful to making survivors feel as if the world was not all bad than were mistrust, avoidance, or outright threats of violence.

Psychological Effects of the Holocaust

Although it was obvious to charity organizations that the survivors needed help getting their health back as well as food, shelter, and jobs, it did not occur to many people that the survivors also needed therapy to overcome the psychological trauma of what they had experienced. Few people realized—not even the survivors—that dealing with the psychological side of living through the Holocaust was important.

When survivors wanted to talk about what had happened to them, they were often discouraged. Some people were worried that talking about the Holocaust would upset survivors. Others felt guilty about not trying to do more to save people while the Holocaust was occurring, so they did not want to hear about it. Helen Epstein, a child of survivors, says that at her synagogue, "all they seemed to be interested in was how we survived and then when we got into the details, they would start talking about the weather because they could not take it. We were like an island."[9]

Others, such as Polish survivor Fela Drybus, did not even try to discuss it with anyone: "For many years I never talked about it, because I could not see how anyone would understand what I had been through."[10] For many years, Alex Gross also did not talk about his experiences in Auschwitz. He says he was afraid he would not be believed "because, quite frankly, who could believe what we'd been through?"[11] He adds that the United States at that time was focused on fighting communism, and had all but forgotten about fascism (the Nazis' oppressive, dictatorial form of government). Homosexual survivors in Germany were afraid to tell anyone what they went through because the Nazi law making homosexuality illegal was still in effect until 1969, when homosexuality was legalized. Many survivors kept their tragedies bottled up inside them or only shared them with their families.

To survive the Holocaust, many people felt as if they had to bury a part of themselves so that what was happening would not hurt them as much. Barbara Steiner, survivor of the Warsaw Ghetto and Majdanek concentration camp, says, "This other person, this *other* Barbara went through all those things, I did not. *I* did not. Because how can you after such a cataclysm, such a destruction of everything, how can you raise children? How can you laugh? How can you enjoy a normal life?"[12]

During the Holocaust, Jewish children were not allowed to experience normal emotions. Crying would make noise and draw Nazi attention. Any sort of behavior that would attract attention was discouraged. Stefanie Seltzer, who was hidden in various places in Poland during the Holocaust, says, "I remember the night that I was told [by the individuals hiding me] that the people in my family had been killed. I went to bed and cried, and I was scolded and beaten, and told not to make any noise."[13]

Some survivors found that even after the Holocaust they were still "closed off" from their emotions. French survivor Robert Deneri says that becoming "hard" helped him survive the concentration camps, but hurt his relationships with his family and friends.[14] Researchers have described survivors who "seemed to have built walls around themselves, who could no longer relate to the idea of 'fun,' who saw themselves as having conquered death but also living it."[15]

Beginning their lives again in a new country, learning a new language, and starting a family kept many survivors so busy that they were able not to think about their Holocaust experiences, at least temporarily. These experiences, however, still had an impact on their lives. In the camps, victims had to hold in their rage toward the Nazis, for fear of losing their lives. Some still felt that rage after liberation and did not know how to deal with it. At a New York conference for children who were hidden during World War II, one woman concluded her story in a shaking voice by saying, "And what I really want to say is that I hate the Germans, I hate the Poles, I hate the Gentiles, and I always will."[16] The anger could be directed inward, causing people to become hard on themselves. It could also be directed outward at Gentiles, Germans, or the world in general. People who realized that they had pent-up anger and tried to do something positive with it—such as helping others or bringing war criminals to justice—felt less frustrated and helpless.

Survivor Syndrome

In the 1960s psychologists became interested in the effects of mass psychological trauma, so they began studying large groups that had survived disasters and other major events. They expected that extreme traumas would create permanent scars. In 1968 Dr. William Niederland identified what he called the survivor syndrome. He said that the main problems for survivors were lasting anxiety and depression. Other symptoms he described were insomnia, night-mares, isolation, and personality changes.[17] Although many may have these symptoms, most survivors dislike the name "survivor syndrome" because they think that it is too general and that it ignores their strengths.

Professor Haim Dasburg describes survivor traits as including excessive anxiety, overprotectiveness, feelings of guilt, grieving, mourning, being psychologically strong, stamina, and being able to identify with others. Many survivors and their children say they have a deep understanding of how injustice affects people, so they never want to sit by while injustices occur. Survivor Franci Solar explains:

> I was quite a frivolous, superficial young girl when the war broke out. But after three years in camp, I learned an enormous amount about human nature, about loyalty, about treachery. It was a very condensed education in coping, in living, and in sorting out a sense of values. You had to decide what was important in life: was it money or posses-sions, or people, or love, or friendship?[18]

Helping people in need and understanding people who are dif-ferent from them are both themes of survivors' post-Holocaust lives. Danish survivor Frode Toft says, "I think it is important that [my son] gets to know as many different peoples and cultures as possible, as early as possible."[19] Dr. Kramer-Freund states after witnessing apartheid when she visited South Africa: "When I saw park benches with 'Whites Only' written on them, that brought back a flood of memories of what had been forbidden to the Jews before the war, and I started to cry."[20]

Holocaust survivors who moved to the United States are often among its most patriotic citizens. They are aware and grateful for the freedoms and rights the United States provides. Czechoslovakian survivor Tomas Radil-Weiss says that survivors everywhere "recog-nize life in peace as one of the highest human values."[21] Rachel Altman, daughter of Polish survivors, says, "My father tells me time and again, fist pounding on the table: 'America is the greatest country that ever was. God bless America.'"[22] Alex Gross was so eager to support the United States and democracy in general that when the United States entered the Korean War, he went to extreme lengths to get himself drafted.

Alex spent two years in the army, which he thought was a good experience. He says he "learned American ways, more of the language, and saved enough money to buy a car."[23] Because he knew seven languages, Alex was assigned to the intelligence department and was not sent to Korea. When he came back home, he went into business with his brother, and then married and started a family.

Starting New Families

As Holocaust survivors began raising their families, memories of their trauma became evident. Following Jewish custom, many survivors named their children after their mothers, fathers, aunts, uncles, daughters, sons, and other family members who had been killed during the Holocaust. Alex, who named his oldest daughter after his mother, says "When we named our children for our lost family, we felt we were bringing them back to life."[24]

Children of survivors often had strong feelings about family members who had been killed. Author Peter Sichrovsky, the son of survivors, writes of his trip to Auschwitz:

> What I saw behind the glass wall of the museum was not a huge mountain of hair, eyeglasses, suitcases, and spoons but the hair of my grandmother, her suitcase, the glasses of my father's little sister. It was a visit to the scene of the crime, and I was looking at the remains of my relatives in order to identify them.[25]

As a teenager, Kim Masters (a child of survivors) wrote a poem about the Nazis and the deaths of her grandparents, that ended, "Creators of hell on earth. I curse you with all my being for this robbery."[26]

Deborah Schwartz, another child of survivors, says she felt that her murdered family was looking down on her, and she hopes that "they felt they had not died in vain. I did not want to let any of them down. I wanted them to be proud of me."[27] Being alive after so many people had died was both a gift and a special burden for Holocaust survivors and their children. Survivors felt guilty that they had been spared when others had not. Their children often believed their lives were a tribute to the dead and a way of easing their parents' suffering.

Reparations

In 1952, in the Luxembourg Accord, West Germany agreed to give Israel $714 million in goods and services because Israel had taken in so many survivors.[28] They also contributed money to Jewish organizations for the support and settlement of Jews outside Israel.

While reparations sound reasonable, in practice it has been controversial and complicated, especially laws concerning reparations for individual survivors. Survivors wanting to claim reparations had to obtain officially designated psychiatrist statements documenting that they had indeed suffered at the hands of Nazi Germany. Survivors were generally wary of German authorities. They felt their experiences did not need to be "okayed."

The psychiatrists themselves did not have much experience with this kind of mass trauma. They thought there would only be short-term effects. At first, they did not expect people who had been young children during the Holocaust to have been affected at all, so they were refused reparations.[29] In general, while many survivors felt they deserved some sort of compensation for the loss of liberty, health, and property that they suffered at the hands of the Nazis, the process for receiving has been long and difficult.

Physical Effects of the Holocaust

Injuries survivors received in the concentration camps affected their health long after the Holocaust. Alex Gross says, "I don't know of any survivor of the death camps who doesn't have lots of health problems."[30] Alex himself suffers from a variety of physical difficulties. A doctor who took an X ray of Alex's leg was surprised to find that Alex had several old fractures that had never been set. Alex says that at the camp the SS guards and kapos (prisoners who were collaborators) kicked people in the leg and tried to break their ankles. When Alex was kicked, he was afraid to show signs of being hurt or even to limp afterward. Hurt or sick prisoners were likely to be sent to the gas chambers. Starvation, malnutrition, beatings, frostbite, and disease affected the survivors physically for years to come.

Post-Traumatic Stress Syndrome

Research on Holocaust survivors has been used to help develop an understanding of how "post-traumatic stress syndrome" affects other groups, such as victims of natural disasters and Vietnam veterans. Sadly, the Holocaust has not been the last genocide of our century. Experiences of Holocaust survivors have also been used to help victims of other atrocities. The government of Rwanda (where the Hutu tribe massacred hundreds of thousands of Tutsi tribe members in 1994), for example, has asked Holocaust survivor groups for help in dealing with the aftermath of the killings. Although the situations were different, the Rwandans dealt with many of the same issues— not knowing what happened to family members, coping with the trauma, making new lives, and remembering the dead.[31]

Holocaust remembrance organizations often feel compelled to speak out against contemporary injustices, especially those which took place in Bosnia and Herzegovina. The United States Holocaust Memorial Council has repeatedly made statements condemning "the brutal campaigns of 'ethnic cleansing' being carried out in the former Yugoslavia. . . . The terrorizing, brutalizing, and murder of innocents, simply because they are members of a particular ethnic or religious group, and primarily for the purpose of removing that group from a geographic area claimed by another group, are acts that are incompatible with all norms of civilized behavior."[32]

The Holocaust had a profound effect not only on those who lived through it, but on many people who were not even born while it was happening. It changed survivors' lives forever. They had to rebuild their emotional, physical, spiritual, and mental health. The Holocaust affected how their children and grandchildren saw the world.

A six-year-old orphan waits for his name to be called at roll call in Buchenwald.

Liberators of the camps had to come to terms with having seen a nightmare worse than any they could have imagined. Those born after the Holocaust—even if they do not know any survivors, liberators, Nazi war criminals, or their children—still live in a world where the Holocaust could happen again. That knowledge alone encourages many to dedicate their lives to making the world more humane.

6 Chapter

THE SEARCH FOR JUSTICE

emember me." Witnesses say these were the last words of a
fourteen-year-old girl who was murdered by notorious concentration camp guard and overseer Hermine Braunsteiner.[1]
The girl was not forgotten, although it took almost thirty years for
Braunsteiner to be tried for her crimes.

After the war, Nazi war criminals who were not captured by the
Allies "went underground" in Europe by assuming new identities or
fleeing to other continents. Some Nazi war criminals found refuge in
the United States. Braunsteiner, for example, hid in Canada, married
an American, and moved to the United States in 1963.[2] She might
have been able to escape accountability for her crimes had it not been
for the dedication of an Austrian and two Americans.

Simon Wiesenthal, Nazi Hunter

The Austrian, Simon Wiesenthal, was a concentration camp survivor
who committed himself to bringing Nazi criminals to justice.
Wiesenthal and his wife lost a total of eighty family members during
the Holocaust. He said, "I am forever asking myself what I can do for
those who have not survived."[3] Wiesenthal felt that working to see

that Nazi murderers were tried for their crimes—or at least that they knew they were being pursued—was his obligation. He wanted future murderers to know that they could not get away with killing.

As the war ended, guards at Mauthausen, the concentration camp where Wiesenthal was imprisoned, took off their uniforms and tried to pass as ordinary Germans outside the camp. Wiesenthal began his work hunting Nazis by helping Americans at the War Crimes Office (WCO) at Mauthausen to identify SS members. The SS was the branch of the Nazi military most responsible for killing Jewish civilians. Wiesenthal continued to work for the War Crimes Office after it moved to Linz, Austria. He also began assisting a newly created Linz organization called the Jewish Committee.

In his work for the Jewish Committee, Wiesenthal made lists of survivors (for people trying to find out what had happened to their families), wrote down survivors' stories, and gathered names of SS criminals and their crimes.[4] Sometimes victims were too upset to talk about what had happened; they wanted to forget and start a new life. Survivors did not always know the names of the SS members who committed atrocities. Wiesenthal, however, carefully collected information from many people.

Wiesenthal and the War Crimes Office were very interested in the outcome of the Nuremberg Trials. If top Nazi leaders were not held responsible for their crimes because they claimed that they were only following orders, then all of the other people Wiesenthal had been collecting evidence against would plead that same defense. Wiesenthal attended the latter part of the trial and noted that the evidence demonstrated the Holocaust was not only the result of hatred, but also of greed (because the Nazis had stolen so much of their victims' possessions, as well as using people for slave labor).[5] Wiesenthal later wondered if some of the stolen wealth was used by Nazis to escape to foreign countries and to pay for lawyers when they were charged for their crimes.

Adolf Eichmann, Organizer
of the Final Solution

Wiesenthal did not believe that all Germans were equally guilty; he devoted his attention to the SS. The man in charge of the executive branch of the SS, Adolf Eichmann, was Wiesenthal's main target. Eichmann had organized the concentration camps and put into motion the Nazis' final solution for the complete extermination of Jews.

Eichmann had been arrested by the Americans at the end of the war, but he had escaped and gone underground. In 1948 Wiesenthal received a tip about Eichmann's whereabouts in Austria. At first Wiesenthal did not take the tip seriously because he had heard many false rumors about Eichmann, but he decided to investigate. He called the Austrian police, who went to the wrong house. By the time they got to the right house, Eichmann was gone. The woman who was there (Veronica Liebl) admitted she had been married to Eichmann, but said they were divorced. She claimed she had not seen him for years.[6]

Although they were divorced, Liebl applied to have Eichmann declared dead (a common practice at the end of the war when people wanted to remarry or to improve their financial situation). Her evidence was an affidavit (signed testimony) from a man named Karl Lukas who claimed he had witnessed Eichmann's death on April 30, 1945, from a gunshot wound. Wiesenthal knew Eichmann had been seen alive after that, so he sent someone to investigate Karl Lukas. His investigator found that Karl Lukas was married to Liebl's sister. This not only ruined Liebl's claim that Eichmann was dead, but increased people's interest in finding Eichmann. It appeared Liebl was trying to have Eichmann declared dead so people would stop looking for him.[7]

Wiesenthal received a tip that Eichmann would be visiting his former wife in Austria at the end of 1949, but when they tried to capture him, someone warned Eichmann and he escaped again. Wiesenthal feared Eichmann fled the country immediately and would never be heard from again. In 1952 Liebl and her sons left Austria, and Wiesenthal believed they had gone to join Eichmann.[8] Wiesenthal thought there was nothing he could do, but through a stroke of luck, he discovered where Eichmann was living.

A man Wiesenthal knew—an Austrian baron who hated Nazis— received a letter from a friend of his in Argentina, who said that Eichmann was living there. Eichmann had changed his name and was working for a water company in Buenos Aires.[9] Wiesenthal shared this information with the Austrian, German, and American governments, and also gave copies of his files to the Israeli consulate and the World Jewish Congress in New York. He was uncertain what would happen because Argentina would not deport Nazi war criminals to countries that wanted to try them for their crimes. Aside from being unconcerned with the Nazi crimes, the Argentinean government officials were concerned about their own futures and wanted to set a precedent that corrupt and criminal officials should have a place of safety.

Five years passed. The Israeli government officials had been too busy with affairs in their own new country to act on the information Wiesenthal had given them, but they had not forgotten. They asked Wiesenthal to investigate Eichmann's assumed name and be certain that it was him. Wiesenthal discovered Eichmann's new name was Ricardo Klement by tracing a Buenos Aires marriage certificate— Liebl and Eichmann had remarried in Argentina. Photographs of Eichmann's four brothers were compared with pictures of Ricardo Klement, and the family resemblance was obvious.

On May 23, 1960, the world found out that the Israelis had captured Ricardo Klement (who admitted to being Adolf Eichmann) and smuggled him out of Argentina to be tried in Jerusalem, Israel. Argentina, angry at Israel for the capture, requested that the United Nations vote to condemn Israel for "violating Argentina's sovereignty" by kidnapping Eichmann.[10]

In spite of the way Eichmann was brought to trial, people around the world were glad to see that he was finally going to be held accountable for his actions. Many people did not know much about the Holocaust before Eichmann's trial. The Eichmann trial, the first televised trial in history, featured hundreds of witnesses who spoke about Eichmann's crimes. It served to draw attention to Nazi war crimes and heightened interest in bringing other war criminals to trial. During the trial Eichmann sat in a glass booth to protect him from potential attacks. He became known as "The Man in the Glass Booth." Eichmann was found guilty and sentenced to death. The trial was a turning point for many Holocaust survivors who, thereafter, found it easier to speak about their experiences.

Anne Frank, Young Writer

In addition to bringing over a thousand important SS officials to trial, Wiesenthal also investigated special projects, such as finding the Gestapo officer who arrested Anne Frank. Anne Frank was a young Jewish girl who, along with her family, hid from the Nazis in an attic in Amsterdam for two years. Someone told the Nazis that Jews were hiding there, and the Frank family was sent to concentration camps. Anne died of typhus in Bergen-Belsen several months before the war's end. Anne's diary was published after the war by her father, the only Frank survivor, and has been translated into myriad languages. Her diary is still being read by children and adults worldwide.

Many Austrian youths had been led to believe by their fellow Austrians, who were trying to cover their World War II Nazi activities, that Anne Frank had never existed. Wiesenthal decided to find the SS officer who arrested her family to prove to them that Anne was a real person. Anne Frank's father, Otto, had survived, but he did not know the officer's name. Paul Kraler, a Dutch friend who had tried to help the Franks when they were arrested, mentioned the officer's name in the appendix of one version of Anne's diary.[11] He did not get the name quite right, but it was enough to go on so, Wiesenthal was able to find the man—Karl Silberbauer. He admitted to arresting Anne Frank and her family. Wiesenthal had accomplished what he set out to do: He established that Anne was a real person who had experienced the events recorded in her diary.

Raoul Wallenberg, Swedish Hero

Wiesenthal was not as lucky with another project—the rescue of Swedish hero Raoul Wallenberg. In January 1944 American President Franklin D. Roosevelt created the War Refugee Board to "forestall the plot of the Nazis to exterminate the Jews and other persecuted minorities of Europe."[12] Wallenberg became an agent of the War Refugee Board in Budapest, Hungary, and was also a diplomat for the Swedish Embassy. Wallenberg was inventive and dedicated in his quest to protect the victims of Nazi persecution. He developed a Swedish passport that protected its bearer by stating that person was immigrating to Sweden and was "in effect, a Swedish citizen."[13]

Wallenberg risked his life on a daily basis in his efforts to prevent Jews from being sent to concentration camps. He would follow trains carrying people who were being deported, pass out his Swedish passports when the Nazis were not looking, and then create a scene about the Nazis taking away protected Swedish citizens. The Nazis would then set their victims free. He bought thirty buildings that he made into "safe houses" for Jews and other threatened people.

Wallenberg's efforts were largely effective until October 1944, when Germany handed the country over to the Nyilas, Hungary's fascists. The Nyilas behaved in an even more bloodthirsty manner than the Germans had in Hungary.[14] Despite the growing dangers, Wallenberg kept saving as many people as he could. When Eichmann ordered thirty thousand Jewish men, women, and children from Budapest to be taken on a 150-mile march across Hungary in November 1944, Wallenberg arrived at the beginning of the second day to issue his Swedish passports to as many people as possible. Susan Tabor, a prisoner who did not manage to get one of the few, precious passports, was so encouraged by his presence that she successfully escaped the march. Tabor said of Wallenberg's visit, "He saved our lives just by caring about us."[15]

Wallenberg's life was threatened by Eichmann and others many times, but he survived the war—only to be seized by the Soviets when they liberated Budapest in January 1945. The Soviets said Wallenberg was killed on his way to Soviet headquarters by Hungarian fascists, but there have always been questions about what really happened to him. In 1971, when Wallenberg's mother asked Simon Wiesenthal to find out what happened to her son, the only ones concerned about Wallenberg were his family. So Wiesenthal took Wallenberg's story to the media, hoping information might surface from the publicity.

After the story was published, Wiesenthal received a phone call from a doctor who said that he had seen Wallenberg in a prison labor camp in Siberia in 1948.[16] Occasionally, Wiesenthal heard from other people who had heard news about Wallenberg's whereabouts, but Wiesenthal was never able to get the Soviets to release Wallenberg or to prove what had happened to him. Wiesenthal did his best to keep Wallenberg's name in the public eye and to make sure he was not sitting forgotten in a Soviet jail cell. He nominated Wallenberg for a Nobel Peace Prize in 1983, but the Nobel is only given to people who are alive, and it could not be proven that Wallenberg was still living.[17] The United States Holocaust Memorial Museum in Washington, D.C., is located on Raoul Wallenberg Place, named in his honor.

Vincent Schiano and Tony DeVito

Taking stories to the press has helped draw attention to forgotten cases, but it has not guaranteed a case would close. In 1964 Wiesenthal told *The New York Times* that a Nazi war criminal, Hermine Braunsteiner, lived in Queens, New York. The German government then asked the United States to deport her back to Germany so she could be tried for her crimes, but the United States did nothing for seven years. It was the responsibility of the U.S. Immigration and Naturalization Service (INS) to revoke Braunsteiner's citizenship and deport her, but they were slow to act and would have even let her stay, had it not been for the determination of INS chief trial lawyer Vincent Schiano.[18]

Schiano refused to drop the matter and asked to be assigned an investigator to help prepare his case. Tony DeVito was appointed the case investigator, and remained on the case despite threats against himself and his family. Mysteriously, evidence "disappeared." When the government was reluctant to pay the money they had agreed to provide for witnesses' expenses, DeVito even collected money by passing around a hat at the INS department every day.[19] He believed that an organization called Odessa was secretly trying to influence the outcome of the trial. Simon Wiesenthal had written about Odessa many years earlier. He had discovered Odessa was a Nazi group whose aim was to protect other Nazis by helping them escape and paying for trial fees. Wiesenthal believed Odessa was probably supported by the money and goods stolen from victims of the Holocaust.

The efforts of Wiesenthal, Schiano, and Tony DeVito to bring Braunsteiner to justice were eventually successful. Braunsteiner voluntarily gave up her citizenship in 1970; her denaturalization case never came to trial. When West Germany asked for Braunsteiner to be deported to their country to be tried for her crimes in 1973, the United States agreed. She was convicted of multiple murders and sentenced to life in prison.

Nazi hunters have overcome many difficulties in their quest to bring the perpetrators of the Holocaust to trial. To succeed, they have triumphed over having a limited amount of funds and resources in dealing with a huge number of cases. In many instances they have also faced a lack of cooperation or interest from the world's governments, including the United States.

7 Chapter

NAZI WAR CRIMINALS AND THE UNITED STATES

The story of how the United States has handled Nazi war criminals within its borders is one that has many embarrassing chapters, but a more encouraging ending. Some war criminals, particularly those who were from East European countries, were allowed into the United States because they passed themselves off as refugees. Others were brought in by the United States government because the government wanted them to work for the United States in their Cold War against the Soviet Union. Simon Wiesenthal has said that the Nazi war criminals who escaped justice were "the real winners of the Cold War."[1]

During World War II the Germans were considered to be ahead of the Allies in their technology, such as the development of rockets. In 1945 it was obvious that the Allies were going to win the war in Europe, but they did not know how long the war against Japan would continue. Some American military people became interested in having German scientists come to the United States to work for them in fighting the Japanese. Since the American public would have been very upset if they knew that members of the German war machine were working for the United States government, the plan was kept secret.[2]

Operation Paperclip

In July 1945 the Joint Chiefs of Staff voted to approve Operation Overcast, which was the plan to bring German scientists into the United States. According to this arrangement up to 350 German and Austrian scientists and technicians could come to the United States for up to one year. They were to come without their families, and they were expected to return to Europe once their work was over.[3]

The war against Japan ended before Operation Overcast got off the ground, however. The United States decided to drop atomic bombs on two Japanese cities in order to hasten the end of the war, which it did. Even so, Operation Overcast was not canceled. Its purpose was changed from fighting Japan to competing militarily with the Soviet Union. Operation Overcast was reapproved in August with the same basic plan and schedule. The program rules permitted only those scientists who were considered "indispensable" (absolutely necessary) and who were not war criminals to join.

The War Department liked the work that the German scientists did so much that it proposed that they stay longer than the time allowed in Operation Overcast. The program was renamed Operation Paperclip because the investigators used paper clips to mark the files of scientists they wanted to keep in the United States. At this time the rules were that anyone who had been an active Nazi could not be included in the program. (Some people in Germany had been forced to join the Nazi party, but they did not take part in Nazi activities.) President Truman okayed Operation Paperclip in September 1946, and it became a top-secret War Department program.[4]

The Joint Intelligence Objectives Agency (JIOA) was in charge of investigating the German scientists who might be brought into the country and was to give information about those scientists to the State Department. In February 1947 the State Department objected to bringing some of the German scientists into the program because of the crimes listed in their files. There was an argument between the State Department and JIOA about the scientists, so the JIOA rewrote the scientists' files—leaving out the crimes—and resubmitted them. The State Department accepted the JIOA files without asking any questions about where the information came from, and they continued to do this for the duration of Operation Paperclip.[5]

United Nations War Crimes Commission

Information about some of the Operation Paperclip scientists could be found in the United Nations War Crimes Commission (WCC) files, but these were closed in 1948 when the WCC shut down. The WCC had gotten a very slow start in collecting material about war criminals—in 1944 even Adolf Hitler was not on the list of war criminals, according to Sir Cecil Hurst, the chair of the WCC.[6] After the war, however, many countries came forward with information they had gathered themselves about crimes that had been committed against their citizens. The United Nations archives, which were kept in the UN building in New York, ended up having eighty-five hundred files containing allegations against thirty-six thousand people.[7] Because the Allies were busy with the Cold War and with rebuilding their countries after World War II, trying all of the Nazi war criminals seemed like it would take too much time, money, and effort, so the files were closed.

In 1987 the United Nations secretary-general, Javier Perez de Cuellar, was pressured to open the files. To open them, he needed permission from the seventeen United Nations members who had originally agreed to close the files. After much discussion the files were finally opened in December of that year. Historians, journalists, investigators, and other interested parties found a wealth of information in the files. For instance, there was a file on former United Nations secretary-general Kurt Waldheim, who was then president of Austria.[8]

Kurt Waldheim

The story of Kurt Waldheim's Nazi past was known by the time the archives were opened, but it was still a bitter irony for many people that a respected diplomat who had led the United Nations had a file in the War Crimes Commission archives.

Until the 1980s Waldheim had managed to keep his activities during 1943–1945 a secret. Early in the decade journalists Shirley Hazzard and Hillel Siedman each realized that Waldheim had a Nazi past, but the story did not attract major interest until 1986. That year an investigator found a 1943 photograph of Waldheim, dressed in a Nazi uniform, standing with two high-level Nazi officers and an Italian officer. One of the Nazi officers had been executed after the war for his war crimes.[9]

Also uncovered was a list made in 1948 of known Nazi war criminals. This list had been compiled by the United States Army from War Crimes Commission information, and included the name "Lieutenant Kurt Waldheim" who was wanted for "murder."[10] When the story of Waldheim's past first began coming out, he completely denied everything. Then he admitted he was there, but said he did not know about the Nazi atrocities. He later said that he had known, but denied having participated in them.[11] In 1987 Waldheim was added to the United States's "Watch List" of people who were to be refused admission into the country.[12]

Klaus Barbie

Another complicated and disturbing story concerned Klaus Barbie, a Nazi war criminal who became a United States spy. Barbie was a ruthless SS officer who sent thousands of people to their deaths and personally tortured and killed many others.[13] His specialty was "intelligence" (collecting military information). In 1947 while one section of the United States Army Counterintelligence Corps (CIC) was looking for Barbie to arrest him as a war criminal, another section of the CIC had already recruited him to spy for the United States in the American-occupied section of Germany.[14]

In 1950 the French tried to get Barbie handed over to them to be tried for crimes against their citizens, but the United States was not sure what to do about Barbie. He had become an embarrassment, and they were also afraid of what he would say if he was turned over (he had actually been spying on the French for the United States). They considered a number of options, but ended up putting Barbie through the "ratline." The ratline was a method for smuggling Nazis such as Barbie into South America.[15]

Barbie changed his name to Klaus Altmann and lived as a protected businessman in Bolivia for twenty years. He moved to Peru in 1971 when his business failed. That same year a German Protestant woman named Beate Klarsfeld heard that a case against Barbie in Munich, Germany, was about to be dropped, and she decided she had to do something. Klarsfeld was married to a Jewish Frenchman who had told her about the Holocaust and how it had affected his family and friends. She did not want to see a major Nazi war criminal go free, so she tried to find out where Barbie was, get the press involved, and gather information about his crimes.[16]

Klarsfeld then decided to go to Peru herself to ask the Peruvian government to send Barbie to France to stand trial. Barbie, however, heard about Klarsfeld's efforts and raced into Bolivia as she was coming. The Bolivian military government refused to give up Barbie. Barbie said that he felt no remorse for what he had done and that he knew too much for any government to do anything to him. The 1980s proved Barbie wrong.

When a new government came to power in Bolivia in 1982, it was not as friendly to Barbie as the previous administration had been. Klarsfeld realized this and encouraged France to renew its extradition request, which it did. The new Bolivian government allowed Barbie to be taken to France. At his French trial Barbie was found guilty and sentenced to life in prison, where he died in 1991.[17]

The U.S. Immigration and Naturalization Service

Before 1980 the official United States government department for handling cases of alleged Nazi war criminals within the United States was the Immigration and Naturalization Service (INS). The INS was in charge of taking away the Nazi criminals' United States citizenship and sending them to another country because the United States did not try them here for their crimes.

The INS did not have a central office for handling Nazi war criminals. Most cases were not pursued, and those that were successfully tried were often overturned later by the Board of Immigration Appeals because they did not want to send people behind the Iron Curtain (to Eastern Europe). The Cold War had another effect on INS efforts—evidence that came from the Soviet Union and Eastern Europe was looked at suspiciously. Because many crimes were committed there, much of the evidence was obtained there also.

This was the situation in 1972 when Representatives Elizabeth Holtzman and Joshua Eilberg began looking into INS treatment of Nazi war criminals in the United States. They were not satisfied with INS efforts and tried to get them to change. The INS had recently been given a list of fifty-nine alleged Nazi war criminals to investigate, so they established a "Project Control Office" to specifically handle Nazi war criminal cases. This office consisted of one man, Sam Zutty, who was not given a staff, budget, or resources.

Three years after the Project Control Office was established, only one case had been brought up. Holtzman and Eilberg were still frustrated with INS and put more pressure on them to change. INS created a "Special Litigation Unit." This new unit turned out to be a disaster—it was very ill-prepared and unsuccessful. In one case they even tried the wrong man. Eilberg and Holtzman concluded that, where Nazi war criminals were concerned, the INS was "hopelessly disorganized and ineffectual."[18]

In 1979 the Office of Special Investigations (OSI) under the Department of Justice was formed. This office took over the Nazi war

criminals cases from the INS. This new organization proved to be more determined and better organized than the INS at pursuing Nazi war criminals living in the United States. The OSI team was frustrated by the amount of time that had passed with no one taking action on these cases, but it did not plan to stop as long as there were still Nazi war criminals living in the United States. The question: "If you are considered to be a valuable worker by the government, are you above the law?" has finally been answered with "no."

Chapter 8

REMEMBRANCE

Joachim Adler, son of a German soldier who fought in World War II, says:

If you want to make something better, you must know the reasons why it was wrong and what has happened. My parents did not know exactly what happened to the Jews. They knew that they disappeared . . . . All the Germans knew that things weren't right for the Jews after Crystal Night. . . . I don't understand why they did not search out what happened to the Jews. . . . I think it's a question in all generations. When I have children [I think] that one day, they will have questions in the same way. They will say to me, 'What did you do?' I try to do now, so later I can say things I did were not wrong.[1]

Why Remember the Holocaust?

There are many reasons for remembering the past and thinking about what happened. In Joachim Adler's case, he wanted to understand why his parents behaved the way they did, and he also used the past as a reminder to himself to behave in ways he could be proud of.

Remembering the Holocaust can be depressing, confusing, and even threatening, because it can contradict our ideas of what human

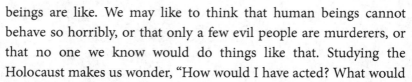

beings are like. We may like to think that human beings cannot behave so horribly, or that only a few evil people are murderers, or that no one we know would do things like that. Studying the Holocaust makes us wonder, "How would I have acted? What would I do if all of the rules I live by were stripped away?"

We find it uncomfortable to think about such things, and may prefer not to. Yet what is the result of forgetting? If you forget the dark side of the human past, then you may be less prepared to deal with it when it crops up again. You may not see the warning signs. You might not realize how important it is to learn about people who are different from you, rather than to just think of them as stereotypes. Or how vital it is to pay attention to what is going on in your government and to work to protect civil rights for everyone.

If you fail to learn about the Holocaust, then your ignorance can be used as a weapon against you. You are vulnerable to being taught a biased version of the past. Hitler himself knew that a country's memories were an important part of its present and future. The Nazi philosophy taught schoolchildren that the Jews had always been evil and would always be evil, and that the Aryan race was superior.

When one country invades another country or when one group wants to destroy another group in its own country, the former country or group usually tries to get rid of the museums, archives, books, writers, and other artists of the latter country or group. These people know the importance of a people's heritage, which is why they target it for destruction.

Some people try to say that the Holocaust never happened, or that not very many people were killed by the Nazis, or that lots of other people have been killed, so the Holocaust isn't very important. These people often try to sound scholarly, but the information that they use to "prove" their points is false.

The Holocaust "revisionists" usually want other people to join their groups, which are based on the idea that they are somehow superior to other groups, including Jews. They try to belittle or deny the Holocaust to make the Nazi ideas appear as though they are not dangerous or evil. They do not want their Nazi heroes to seem like evil soldiers who planned and carried out the deaths of millions of innocent people. The revisionists especially like to put their information on World Wide Web sites on the Internet, because they can write anything and say it is true. Other people may think that the Holocaust did not occur just because they have not learned anything about it. Holocaust remembrance is important, so people can learn the truth and know that it happened.

Even though the Holocaust is an abominable part of our human heritage, there are lessons to be learned from it. Learning those lessons is the reason for not forgetting. As Jonathan Blumen writes in his essay "What I Learned from Auschwitz": "It is not enough merely to remember the past; one must remember the truth, analyze it, derive rules from it and desire to act."[2]

The Holocaust is difficult to write or talk about because words don't seem enough to express the horror. Even people who lived through the death camps or who liberated them cannot always find a way to describe the experience. As Holocaust survivor and author Elie Wiesel says, "I know there are no words for it, so all I can try to do is to communicate the incommunicability of the event."[3] So one of the dilemmas of Holocaust remembrance is to be able to do it justice.

Another challenge of remembering the Holocaust is that we must think of the murdered victims as individuals, not just as numbers, but at the same time we must remember that huge numbers of people died. Communicating both the enormity of the Holocaust and its personal aspects is difficult. Also, as people discuss the Holocaust, they want to be realistic, but they don't want their listeners to become overwhelmed and numb to the tragedy. Michael Berenbaum of the United States Holocaust Memorial Museum says, "The Holocaust cannot be allowed to numb us to evil, but it must sensitize us and alarm us. It must sharpen our insights into the importance of human rights and human dignity everywhere."[4]

One more problem of remembrance is how to tell how horribly the Nazis and their supporters behaved without making them seem monstrous or superhuman. They sunk to the bottom of how human beings can behave, lower than we even realized that people could, but they were still human beings. The danger of forgetting this is that we may think that it will not happen again because only especially evil people can behave that way.

Remembering Heroes

Creating a museum, monument, or work of art featuring such a complex subject as the Holocaust is very difficult, but many people around the world have felt it was necessary. One of the largest is the government-sponsored Holocaust memorial in Israel. Called the Yad Vashem, the Israeli memorial is a group of museums, monuments, and research and resource centers. In their effort to remember, they have gathered a huge amount of documentation and testimony about the Holocaust in their library and archives. One of their most famous sections is the tribute to non-Jews who risked their lives to save Jews during the Holocaust. Along the "Avenue of the Righteous," each carob tree that lines the walk of honor is dedicated to a rescuer.

Having museums and memorials to rescuers or resistance fighters is a popular way to remember the Holocaust. Some people think that it is deceptive to concentrate on the heroes of the Holocaust because there were so few of them. They believe that the true picture of the Holocaust becomes distorted this way, and the lessons of the Holocaust may be lost. Others, however, believe that remembering the heroes can be positive if the other lessons are kept in mind. They feel we must honor the rescuers who bravely went against the mainstream to follow their conscience and the resistance fighters who stood up to evil against all odds.

In situations where people are afraid for themselves, they may let horrible things happen to other people and not get involved. Even though most non-Jews in Germany did not do anything to stop the Holocaust, and many joined or helped the Nazis in various ways, that was not the only way to live. The people who actively tried to help the Jews prove that there is always a choice to be made, no matter how dangerous the situation is. They show that individuals can be willing to risk personal harm to aid others because their conscience tells them it is the right thing to do.

Varian Fry is an American who was awarded the title "Righteous Among Nations" by Yad Vashem. He joined the Emergency Rescue Committee to help Jews during World War II. In 1940 he was given 200 visas by the United States to help rescue people in southern France. The French collaborationist government was voluntarily turning over Jews to the Nazis. Like Raoul Wallenberg, Fry was creative, bold, and dedicated, and he managed to save four thousand people. The French governments expelled Fry from France in 1941 and he returned to the United States. In the 1960s, however, the French government awarded him its Legion of Honor medal, one of the highest honors France can bestow.[5]

There are Holocaust remembrances for heroes from all over the world. Most heroes lived in the countries occupied by the Nazis, but some, like Varian Fry, did not, and some even lived in countries that were allied with Germany. For instance, Chiune and Yukiko Sugihara, a Japanese diplomat and his wife, risked their careers and futures to help more than six thousand Jews escape from the Nazis. The Sugiharas' heroism has been celebrated in museum exhibits and books.

Other heroes now honored were brave people who tried to help the Jews by letting the world know what was happening to them. Jan Karski, a member of the Polish underground, came to London in 1942 to tell the Allies about the Holocaust and demand help.[6] American photographer Therese Bonney made "truth raids" to Europe to take pictures during World War II. She said, "I go forth alone, try to get the truth and then bring it back and try to make others face it and do something about it."[7]

The Ghetto Fighters House in Israel spotlights Jewish efforts to fight the Nazis during the Holocaust. The museum focuses on individual resisters, community rebellions, ghetto uprisings, and youth resistance movements. In addition to exhibits, they also have a study center, archives, and art museum. Many pieces in the art collection were made in the ghettos and the concentration camps during the Holocaust; others were created by survivors after liberation.

During the Holocaust, even though concentration camp victims were suffering horribly, some still managed to create art. They used art to make a record of what was happening and to express their feelings about it. Others drew pictures of imagined worlds where life was better or of the future the way they hoped it would be. Some wrote poems or kept journals. Charlotte Delbo, a survivor of the concentration camp Auschwitz, says:

> When I would recite a poem, when I would tell the comrades beside me what a novel or a play was about while we went on digging in the muck of the swamp, it was to keep myself alive, to preserve my memory, to remain me, to make sure of it. Never did that succeed in nullifying the moment I was living through, not for an instant. To think, to remember was a great victory over the horror, but it never lessened it.[8]

Concentration camp artists used whatever materials they could find and saved their work by hiding it. If their art was found by Nazis or kapos, they could have been punished with death. The concentration camp administrators did not want records of the camps to exist.

One of the most widely known memorials in the world was created during World War II. It is Poland's Warsaw Ghetto Monument. This monument symbolizes both celebration and grief because it represents the Jewish bravery in resisting the Nazis and the destruction of the Warsaw Jews. The Warsaw Ghetto Monument was created by sculptor Nathan Rapoport and was unveiled on April 19, 1948, the fifth anniversary of the Warsaw Ghetto Uprising.[9]

The Earliest Holocaust Memorials

The first monuments to the Holocaust were the concentration camps themselves. In July 1944, when the Soviets found the Majdanek camp, they turned it into a memorial. In 1947 the Polish government stated that Auschwitz-Birkenau would be preserved as a memorial to the millions of Polish dead.[10] The old concentration camps are visited every year by thousands of people who want to see where the destruction took place and pay tribute to the people who suffered there.

The memorialized camps have also occasionally been the focal point for activities by people who model themselves after the Nazis (neo-Nazis), such as an incident at the Buchenwald memorial in 1996. According to eyewitness accounts, twenty-two right-wing skinheads roared through the site "threatening to burn a woman supervisor to death, shouting 'Sieg Heil,' throwing rocks at buildings and giving the Nazi salute." In response, about five hundred Germans held a peaceful anti-Nazi protest in Buchenwald two weeks later.[11] Neo-Nazi violence proves once again that we should not forget. What has happened in the past can happen again.

In another act of remembrance, thousands of Jewish teens and others come together every year from all over the world for the "March of the Living." First, the group visits cities in Poland where Jews had thriving communities before World War II. They learn about the hundreds of Jewish schools, synagogues, and entire communities that were destroyed during the war. Then, they visit concentration camps in Poland and take part in a march from Auschwitz to Birkenau on Holocaust Remembrance Day (*Yom HaShoa*). The march mirrors the one that so many children and adults took on the way to their deaths, but this one is a "March of the Living." These marchers are modern teens who try to understand the pain and tragic loss of the Holocaust.

This experience helps these students think from the point of view of the concentration camp prisoners, and made one woman ask herself, "Would I have had the strength to survive this? And if I had indeed been strong enough, would I have had the will to live in this Hell?"[12] The last portion of the "March of the Living" takes the students to Israel to participate in Remembrance Day and Independence Day observances there.

Remembrance Takes Many Forms

The United States government sponsored the creation of the a Holocaust museum to be built in a country that was not directly affected by the Holocaust. In 1980 the United States Congress unanimously established the United States Holocaust Memorial Council for the purpose of creating a memorial to the millions who were killed in the Holocaust. The architect of the museum, James Ingo Freed, visited the preserved concentration camps in Europe because he wanted the United States museum to recreate the feeling of being in a camp.[13] The United States Holocaust Memorial Museum was opened on the fiftieth anniversary of the Warsaw Ghetto Uprising (April 1993).

Visitors to the museum over the age of thirteen start on the top floor with exhibits about Jewish life before the Holocaust; moving to the lower floors, visitors see exhibits that trace the Holocaust years with artifacts, photographs, documentaries, and oral histories. The information in this part of the museum is considered too graphic for young children, so kids from eight to thirteen see a special exhibit called "Daniel's Story: Remember the Children." Based on the experiences of real Jewish children and their families, "Daniel's Story" tells the story of a fictional young boy's experiences during the Holocaust. The exhibit includes original photographs and video from the Holocaust as well as interactive sections.

People remember the Holocaust in all kinds of ways—with museums, monuments, and memorials, on marches, through books, movies, and paintings, and many other media. For example, Art Spiegelman, the son of Holocaust survivors, used an unusual art form to tell his family's story—the comic book. Spiegelman said, "I entered my work so gingerly. There were so many ways to do it that are disrespectful to the ghosts."[14] In his two-book series, called *Maus*, Spiegelman makes all the characters animals (the Jews are mice, the Nazis are cats, the Poles are pigs, and so on). But Spiegelman tells a complicated story even so. He shows what his parents' lives were like before, during, and after the Holocaust, and how it affected his relationship with them. Spiegelman won a Pulitzer Prize for *Maus*.

The B'nai B'rith Jewish service organization arranges "Unto Every Person There Is A Name" ceremonies in the United States every April. All across the country hundreds of groups come together to read aloud the names of the 6 million Jews killed in the Holocaust. Name-reading programs are also sponsored in many other countries. Tommy Baer, the international president of B'nai B'rith, says, "This program restores some dignity to those who were stripped of their identities and robbed of their lives. The Nazis killed so many people and tried to obliterate any memory, that even this effort is insufficient to recall every victim."[15]

The Anne Frank House in Holland, which is where Anne Frank and her family hid during the Holocaust before they were betrayed, is a popular memorial center. It reminds the Dutch citizens both of how courageous and how treacherous people can be. Around the corner from the Anne Frank House is a monument to the homosexual people who were murdered by the Nazis. The monument is a large marble triangle (a symbol the Nazis forced their victims to wear to identify them) traced into the ground. One corner points in the direction of Anne Frank House; another to the local Gay Coalition offices; and the last to Holland's National Monument.[16]

Anne Frank's legacy is far-reaching. Teenagers everywhere relate to the feelings she expressed in her diary. Her father, Otto, was contacted by many teens whose lives were changed by Anne's writings. When he visited Israel, Otto met a Japanese Christian youth group who began crying and hugging him when the youths discovered who he was. They later visited him at his home in Switzerland, and one member of the group worked to create the first Holocaust museum in Hiroshima, Japan.[17]

Lessons from the Holocaust

When people memorialize the Holocaust, they remind us that people are capable of going to war against children and adults not because of anything they have done, but because they are different. This lesson is as true today as it was more than fifty years ago when the Holocaust began.

Professors Sander Gilman and Steven Katz, coeditors of a book of essays entitled *Anti-Semitism in Times of Crisis*, say that when a country is having a crisis, people look for someone to blame, and ethnic hatred rears its ugly head.[18] This tendency is why tolerance and respect for difference need to be part of a country's deeply held values, so that in times of crisis, people do not lose sight of the humanity of all its citizens. In a speech to Holocaust survivors, American president Ronald Reagan said, "We recognize that for freedom to prosper, it must be engraved on our character, so that when confronted with fundamental choices, we will do what is right, because that is our way."[19]

Rescuers versus Bystanders

Professors Pearl and Samuel Oliner studied people who acted as rescuers and non-rescuers during the Holocaust to see "what led ordinary men and women to risk their lives on behalf of others."[20] They found that altruistic people (rescuers) tended to have "extensive" personalities and non-rescuers tended to have "constricted" personalities.[21]

The Oliners describe rescuers' personalities as caring strongly for those outside their family circle and possessing a sense of responsibility for others' welfare. They describe rescuers' parents as being nurturing role models. Rescuers' parents tended to explain to their children why they should behave morally and discussed the consequences of their actions. They encouraged their children to be confident, trusting, and responsible. They helped their children be more comfortable in dealing with people who were different from themselves and to be open to new experiences. When other people are threatened, children raised with these values are more likely to help.[22]

Toby Mostysster, daughter of Polish survivors, was deeply moved by the great danger her parents' rescuer, Rybokova, faced to protect her parents. She says, "I learned that there was a peasant woman called Rybokova, who allowed my parents to hide in her attic and gave them food—this, in the middle of the war, when she and her children were themselves often hungry, when any prying and malicious eye might have informed on her for a pound of salt or for pleasure, and when, had the Germans or even her own countrymen caught her, she and her family would surely have died a most terrible death."[23]

Parents whose children have constricted (bystander) personalities, on the other hand, tend to stereotype outsiders and fear the unknown. They do not provide reasons for behavior and generally use punishment to discipline their children. The bystanders' parents believe social relationships are centered on usefulness ("How can this interaction help me?") rather than on caring. Constricted people tend to feel insecure, vulnerable, and threatened. When other people are threatened, bystanders are likely to turn the other way or even join the threatening group.[24]

Teaching Tolerance

Today many people in the United States and around the world are working in the area of tolerance education. For instance, Facing History and Ourselves is a nonprofit foundation that helps schools teach about racism and anti-Semitism in the history of the United States and abroad. They believe that if we deny "our students access to this history, we fail to honor their potential to confront, to cope, and to make a difference today and in their futures."[25]

One of the Facing History and Ourselves resource books quotes a thought-provoking letter that a principal sent the teachers at his school on the first day of the school year:

Dear Teacher:
I am a survivor of a concentration camp. My eyes saw what no man should witness:

Gas chambers built by learned engineers.

Children poisoned by educated physicians.

Infants killed by trained nurses.

Women and babies shot and burned by high school and college graduates.

So, I am suspicious of education.

My request is: Help your students become human. Your efforts must never produce learned monsters, skilled psychopaths, educated Eichmanns.

Reading, writing, arithmetic are important only if they serve to make our children more humane.

Approximately 11 million people died in the Holocaust. That number is so huge that it is impossible for us to picture every single person who died. We can't imagine them all, but we must not forget them either. For their sakes, and for ours too.

CHRONOLOGY

November 1917

Great Britain makes the Balfour Declaration (supporting a Jewish national home in Palestine).

January 1933

Hitler becomes chancellor of Germany.

March 1933

The German Parliament gives Hitler dictatorial powers.

June 1933

At Dachau, Hitler opens the first concentration camp.

August 1934

German President von Hindenberg dies, and Hitler becomes the führer.

September 1935

Hitler publishes the Nuremberg Laws, depriving Jews of their civil rights.

February 1936

The Nazi Gestapo is placed above the law.

August 1936

The Olympic Games begin in Berlin, Germany's capital.

March 1938

Germany occupies Austria.

July 1938

A League of Nations conference held in Evian, France, to consider helping Jews who are fleeing the Third Reich results in inaction.

November 9, 1938

Kristallnacht ("Night of Broken Glass") occurs.

March 1939

Germany invades Czechoslovakia.

September 1939

Germany invades Poland, starts war with Great Britain and France.

October 1939

Hitler starts "euthanasia program" (killing people who are hospitalized); Great Britain passes the "White Paper" (drastically limiting Jewish immigration into Palestine).

April 1940

Germany invades Denmark and Norway.

May 1940

Germany invades France, Belgium, Holland, and Luxembourg.

November 1940

Hungary, Romania, and Slovakia become Nazi allies.

March 1941

Germany occupies Bulgaria.

April 1941

Germany occupies Yugoslavia and Greece.

June 1941

Germany invades Russia; Ghettos and concentration camps are established in Poland.

December 7, 1941

Japan bombs Pearl Harbor. December 8, 1941

The United States enters World War II.

January 1942

Mass killings using the poison gas Zyklon-B begin at the concentration camp Auschwitz-Birkenau in Poland.

January 20, 1942

Nazi leaders construct the "Final Solution," a plan to kill all the Jewish people in Europe at the Wannsee Conference.

January 1943

Hitler orders all Gypsies arrested and taken to extermination camps.

✕━━━━✕━━━━✕━━━━✕━━━━✕━━━━✕━━━━✕

April 1943

Warsaw (Poland) Ghetto uprising occurs; United Nations War Crimes Commission begins keeping a list of Nazi war criminals.

March 1944

Germany occupies Hungary.

June 6, 1944

The Allies invade Normandy, France (D-day).

July 1944

Swedish diplomat Raoul Wallenberg arrives in Hungary.

August 1944

Anne Frank's family is caught in Amsterdam and sent to Auschwitz.

August 23, 1944

Paris, France, is liberated.

January 1945

Soviets liberate Budapest, Hungary; Raoul Wallenberg disappears; Soviets liberate Warsaw, Poland.

February 1945

Allies hold Yalta Conference.

April 1945

Buchenwald, Auschwitz, and Dachau concentration camps are liberated.

April 30, 1945

Hitler commits suicide.

May 1945

Mauthausen concentration camp is liberated.

May 7, 1945

V-E day (Victory in Europe).

July 1945

United States Joint Chiefs of Staff propose to bring German scientists to the United States.

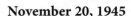

November 20, 1945
Nuremberg Trials begin.

October 1, 1946
Nuremberg Trials' verdicts are announced.

1947
There are still 850,000 displaced people in Europe.

November 29, 1947
UN votes to create a separate Jewish state in Palestine (Israel).

May 15, 1948
Creation of Israel is announced; Arab countries invade Israel; UN convention defines *genocide.*

January 1949
A truce is declared in the Arab-Israeli war.

September 1952
West Germany agrees to pay reparations to Nazi victims.

May 1960
Eichmann is captured in Argentina and brought to Israel for trial.

1979
The U.S. Department of Justice establishes the Office of Special Investigations (OSI).

1986
Holocaust survivor and author Elie Wiesel wins Nobel Peace Prize.

1987
Klaus Barbie (the "Butcher of Lyons") is tried in France for his crimes.

1993
United States Holocaust Memorial Museum opens in Washington, D.C.

CHAPTER NOTES

Overview of the Holocaust

1. Anton Gill, *The Journey Back from Hell* (New York: William Morris & Company, 1988), p. 224.

Chapter 1. Liberation: A Survivor's View

1. Interview with Alex Gross conducted by the author, October 1996, Atlanta, Ga.

2. Ibid.

3. Martin Gilbert, *The Holocaust* (New York: Henry Holt, 1985), p. 793.

4. Ibid., pp. 786–787.

5. Simon Wiesenthal, *Justice Not Vengeance* (New York: Grove Weidenfeld, 1989), p. 30.

6. Elie Wiesel, *Night* (New York: Bantam Books, 1982), p. 32.

7. Dwight Eisenhower, *Crusade in Europe* (Garden City, N.Y.: Doubleday & Co., 1948), p. 451.

8. William Scott, *World War II Veteran Remembers the Horror of the Holocaust* (unpublished, no page numbers).

9. Ibid.

10. Ibid.

11. South Carolina ETV Holocaust Forum, "American Soldiers See the Camps," Lesson 9 <http://www.scetv. stats.sc.us/scetv/les9.html>.

12. David A. Adler, *We Remember the Holocaust* (New York: Henry Holt, 1989), p. 90.

13. Charles V. Ferree, "My Holocaust Experiences," Cybrary of the Holocaust, Liberators testimony <http:// www.remember.org>.

14. Sue M. Hanover and David R. Blumenthal, ed., *Emory Studies on the Holocaust: An Interfaith Inquiry* vol. 2, (Atlanta: Emory University, 1988), p. 23.

15. Alex Gross interview.

16. Charles Ferree, "Displaced Persons Camp (Law and Order for the Property Owners At Least)" Cybrary of the Holocaust, Liberators testimony <http://www. remember.org>.

17. Gilbert, p. 819.

18. Anton Gill, *The Journey Back from Hell* (New York: William Morris & Company, 1988), p. 6.

Chapter 2. Victory in Europe

1. Basil Collier, *The Second World War: A Military History* (Gloucester, Mass.: Peter Smith, 1978), p. 392.

2. Martin Gilbert, *The Holocaust* (New York: Henry Holt & Company, 1985), p. 684.

3. Peter Hoffman, *The History of the German Resistance 1933–1945* (Cambridge, Mass.: The MIT Press, 1977), pp. 375–377.

4. Robert Leckie, *Delivered from Evil* (New York: Harper & Row Publishers, 1987), p. 732.

5. Robert Abzug, *Inside the Vicious Heart* (New York: Oxford University Press, 1985), p. 5.

6. Gilbert, p. 711.

7. Leckie, pp. 722–723.

8. Anton Gill, *The Journey Back from Hell* (New York: William Morris & Company, 1988), p. 312.

9. Ibid., p. 218.

10. "The Army Nurse Corps of World War II," World War II: The World Remembers, Patch American High School Home Page <http://192.253.114.31/D-Day/GVPT_stuff/Nurse/Nurse_page3.html>.

11. Gilbert, p. 695.

12. Abzug, p. 22.

13. Omar N. Bradley, *A Soldier's Story* (New York: Henry Holt, 1951), p. 539.

14. Abzug, p. 31.

15. Ibid., p. 58.

16. Ibid., p. 103.

17. Ibid., p. 74.

18. Howard Greenfeld, *Hidden Children* (New York: Ticknor & Fields, 1993), p. 35.

Chapter 3. Trials of Major Nazi Leaders at Nuremberg

1. Airey Neave, *Nuremberg: A Personal Record of the Trial of the Major Nazi War Criminals in 1945-6* (London: Hodder and Stoughton, 1978), p. 243.

2. Ibid., p. 24.

3. Joseph E. Persico, *Nuremberg: Infamy on Trial* (New York: Penguin Books, 1994), p. 135.

4. "War Crimes," Grolier Interactive <http://www. grolier.com/wwii/wwii_warcrimes.html>.

5. Ibid.

6. Ibid.

7. Neave, p. 238

8. Neave, p. 256.

9. Victor H. Bernstein, *Final Judgment: The Story of Nuremberg* (New York: Boni & Gaer, 1947), pp. 15-16.

10. Ben S. Austin, "The Nuremberg Trials: The Defendants and Verdicts" <http://www.mtsu.edu/ ~baustin/trials3.html>.

11. Robert Jackson's closing speech, Court TV Law Center <http://www.courttv.com/casefiles/serb/trial>.

12. Eugene Davidson, *The Trial of the Germans* (New York: The Macmillan Company, 1966), p. 2.

13. Bernstein, p. 4.

14. "War Crimes," Grolier Interactive <http://www.grolier.com/wwii/wwii_warcrimes.html>.

15. Colin Soloway and Kevin Whitelaw, "NATO Finally Goes After Indicted War Criminals," *U.S. News & World Report*, July 21, 1997, p. 43.

Chapter 4. Finding a Home: The Creation of Israel

1. Geoffrey Moore, ed., *Great American Poets: Robert Frost* (New York: Clarkston N. Potter, Inc., 1986), p. 24.

2. Howard Sachar, *A History of Israel from the Rise of Zionism to Our Time* (New York: Alfred A. Knopf, 1996), p. 4.

3. Ronnie S. Landau, *The Nazi Holocaust* (Chicago: Ivan R. Dee, 1944), pp. 37–38.

4. Ibid., p. 13.

5. *Israel* (Amsterdam: Time-Life Books, 1986), p. 56.

6. Ibid., p. 60.

7. Sol Scharfstein, *Understanding Israel* (Hoboken, N.J.: KTAV Publishing House, Inc., 1944), p. 98.

8. Ibid., p. 100.

9. Sachar, p. 237.

10. Noah Lucas, *The Modern History of Israel* (New York: Praeger Publishers, 1975), p. 225.

11. Sachar, p. 263.

12. Ibid., p. 270.

13. Ibid., p. 276.

14. Bernard Postal and Henry W. Levy, *And the Hills Shouted for Joy* (New York: David McKay Co., Inc., 1973), pp. 17–19.

15. Postal and Levy, pp. 19-20.

16. Neil Grant, *The Partition of Palestine, 1947* (New York: Franklin Watts, Inc., 1973), p. 78.

Chapter 5. Survivors Starting Over

1. Alex Gross interview, October 15, 1996.

2. Anton Gill, *The Journey Back from Hell* (New York: William Morris & Company, 1988), p. 8.

3. Alex Gross interview.

4. Dina Wardi, *Memorial Candles* (London: Routledge, 1992), p. 8.

5. Alex Gross interview.

6. Ibid.

7. Helen Epstein, *Children of the Holocaust* (New York: G. P. Putnam's Sons, 1979), p. 98.

8. Gill, p. 213.

9. Epstein, p. 157.

10. Gill, p. 142.

11. Alex Gross interview.

12. The Staff of the *Washington Post, Holocaust: The Obligation to Remember* (Washington, D.C.: *Washington Post*, 1983), p. 28.

13. Howard Greenfeld, *Hidden Children* (New York: Ticknor & Fields, 1993), p. 91.

14. Gill, p. 314.

15. Epstein, p. 107.

16. Carol Rittner and John K. Roth, *Different Voices: Women and the Holocaust* (New York: Paragon House, 1993), p. 371.

17. Ibid., p. 104.

18. Epstein, pp. 166–167.

19. Gill, p. 135.

20. Ibid., p. 217.

21. Tomas Radil-Weiss, "Men in Extreme Conditions: Some Medical and Psychological Aspects of the Auschwitz Concentration Camp," *Psychiatry*, vol. 46, August 1983, p. 269.

22. Rittner and Roth, p. 369.

23. Alex Gross interview.

24. Ibid.

25. Peter Sichrovsky, *Strangers in Their Own Land* (New York: Basic Books, 1986), p. 161.

26. *Washington Post* Staff, p. 12.

27. Epstein, p. 302.

28. Ibid., p. 99.

29. Epstein, p. 100–101.

30. Alex Gross interview.

31. Alissa Kaplan, "Holocaust Survivors in Israel Help Rwanda Deal With Genocide," *Jewish Telegraphic Agency*, November 20, 1995.

32. "Statement by the United States Holocaust Memorial Council on the Carnage in the Former Yugoslavia," August 3, 1995.

Chapter 6. The Search for Justice

1. Howard Blum, *Wanted! The Search for Nazis in America* (New York: Simon & Schuster, Inc., 1977), p. 16.

2. Ibid., p.12.

3. Simon Wiesenthal, *Justice Not Vengeance* (London: Weidenfeld and Nicolson, 1989), p. 352.

4. Joseph Wechsburg, ed., *The Murderers Among Us* (New York: McGraw Hill Book Company, 1967), p. 51.

5. Iris Noble, *Nazi Hunter: Simon Wiesenthal* (New York: Julian Messner, 1979), p. 45.

6. Wiesenthal, p. 69.

7. Ibid., p. 70.

8. Wechsburg, p. 122.

9. Ibid., p. 123.

10. Alan Levy, *The Wiesenthal File* (New York: William B. Eerdmans Publishing Company, 1993), p.134.

11. Wiesenthal, pp. 337–338.

12. Levy, p. 147.

13. Ibid., p. 150.

14. Martin Gilbert, *The Holocaust* (New York: Henry Holt, 1985), p. 751.

15. Levy, p. 160.

16. Ibid., p. 183.

17. Ibid., p. 191.

18. Blum, p. 13.

19. Ibid., p. 18.

Chapter 7. Nazi War Criminals and the United States

1. Joseph Wechsburg, ed., *The Murderers Among Us* (New York: McGraw Hill Book Company, 1967), p. 87.

2. Charles Ashman and Robert J. Wagman, *The Nazi Hunters* (New York: Pharos Books, 1988), p. 211.

3. Clarence G. Lasby, *Project Paperclip* (New York: Atheneum, 1971), p. 89.

4. Christopher Simpson, *Blowback* (New York: Weidenfeld & Nicolson, 1988), p. 35.

5. Ibid., pp. 36-38.

6. Ashman and Wagman, p. 60.

7. Ibid., p. 49

8. Stanley Meisler, *The United Nations: The First Fifty Years* (New York: The Atlantic Monthly Press, 1995), p. 193.

9. Ashman and Wagman, p. 85.

10. Ibid., p. 88.

11. Meisler, p. 190.

12. Ibid., p. 202.

13. Erhard Dabringhaus, *Klaus Barbie* (Washington, D.C.: Acropolis Books Ltd., 1984), p. 35.

14. Ibid., p. 132.

15. Ibid., p. 176.

16. Ashman and Wagman, p. 148.

17. Ibid., p. 152.

18. Ibid., p. 192.

Chapter 8. Remembrance

1. Studs Terkel, *The Good War* (New York: Ballantine Books, 1993), pp. 579–580.

2. Jonathan Blumen, "What I Learned From Auschwitz" <http://www.spectacle.org/695/essay.html>.

3. Elie Wiesel interview, June 29, 1996 <http://www.achievement.org/autodoc/page/wie0int-1>.

4. Marcia D. Horn, "Holocaust's Memory Mustn't Fade," *Roanoke Times & World News*, August 20, 1996.

5. AP article from Jerusalem <gopher://dept.english.upenn.edu:70/00/Courses/Holocaust/News/varian-fry>.

6. *Facing History and Ourselves Holocaust and Human Behavior Resource Book* (Brookline, Mass.: Facing History and Ourselves National Foundation, Inc., 1994), pp. 367–368.

7. "Women Come to the Front," Library of Congress Exhibit, Washington, D.C.

8. Carol Rittner and John K. Roth, *Different Voices: Women and the Holocaust* (New York: Paragon House, 1993), p. 330.

9. James E. Young, *The Art of Memory: Holocaust Memorials in History* (New York: The Jewish Museum, 1994), p. 25.

10. Ibid., p. 23.

11. Reuter article from Buchenwald <gopher:// dept.english.upenn.edu:70/00/Courses/Holocaust/News/buchenwald-protest>.

12. Jane Forness, "We Should Never Forget" <http://www.mcl.ucsb.edu/nexus/dat/apr27/o3.html>.

13. Eleanor H. Ayer, *The United States Holocaust Memorial Museum* (New York: Dillon Press, 1994), p. 15.

14. Fred Bruning, "The Problem with Schindler's List," *Maclean's*, April 25, 1994.

15. "Across U.S., Millions of Holocaust Victims Will Be Remembered in Community-Wide Events," B'nai B'rith Organization, Washington, D.C.

16. Young, p. 31.

17. Cara Wilson, *Love, Otto: The Legacy of Anne Frank* (Kansas City: Andrews and McMeel, 1995), p. 135.

18. Carole Stone, "Ethnic Hatred Is a Constant in Times of Social Crisis, Professors Say," *Cornell Chronicle*, August 5, 1993.

19. The Staff of the *Washington Post, Holocaust: The Obligation to Remember* (Washington, D.C.: *Washington Post*, 1983), p. 22.

20. Samuel P. Oliner and Pearl M. Oliner, *The Altruistic Personality* (New York: The Free Press, 1988), title.

21. Ibid., p. 251.

22. Ibid., p. 250.

23. Lucy Y. Steinitz with David M. Szony, eds., *Living after the Holocaust* (New York: Bloch Publishing Company, 1975), pp. 7–8.

24. Oliner, p. 251.

25. *Facing History and Ourselves Holocaust and Human Behavior Resource Book*, p. xix.

GLOSSARY

Allies—The nations (Great Britain, United States, Soviet Union, and France) fighting against the Axis powers (Germany, Italy, and Japan) during World War II.

collaborator—A person from an occupied country who aided the Nazis.

concentration camp—Prison in which "enemies of the Third Reich" were kept.

conspiracy—A common plan to commit a crime in the future.

crematorium—Oven for reducing dead bodies to ashes (method of getting rid of murdered people).

crimes against humanity—Committing crimes against people, such as murder, deportation, and religious persecution, regardless of whether the action violated domestic law at the time.

crimes against peace—Planning, preparing, initiating, or waging a war of aggression.

deportation—Forced relocation of Jews and Gypsies to ghettos, concentration camps, labor camps, or death camps (killing centers).

final solution—Nazi term for killing all the Jews in Europe.

gas chamber—Sealed rooms in death camps where people were poisoned by gas or carbon monoxide.

genocide—The deliberate and systematic destruction of a religious, racial, national, or cultural group.

ghetto—In occupied Europe, a closed-off section of a city where Jews (and sometimes Gypsies) were forced to live until they were deported to concentration camps.

Gypsies—A nomadic people believed to have come originally from northwest India. Approximately five hundred thousand Gypsies are thought to have died at the hands of the Nazis.

kapo—Prisoner in charge of a group of inmates in Nazi concentration camps. Many kapos had been prisoners in jails and were released solely to help run the camps.

SS—(Short for Schutzstaffel) Nazi military group known for carrying out the killing of the Jews.

Third Reich—Official name of the Nazi German state.

war crimes—Violations of international agreements governing the conduct of war, such as mistreatment of prisoners, murder, or forced labor of occupied civilian populations.

Zionism—Movement to found Jewish homeland in Palestine/Israel.

Zyklon-B—The poison gas used by Nazis in the death camp gas chambers to commit mass murder.

FURTHER READING

Abzug, Robert. *Inside the Vicious Heart*. New York: Oxford University Press, Inc., 1985.

Adler, David. *We Remember the Holocaust*. New York: Henry Holt, 1989.

Ashman, Charles, and Robert J. Wagman. *The Nazi Hunters*. New York: Pharos Books, 1988.

Ayer, Eleanor. *The United States Holocaust Memorial Museum: America Keeps the Memory Alive*. New York: Dillon Press, 1994.

Blum, Howard. *Wanted! The Search for Nazis in America*. New York: Simon & Schuster, Inc., 1989.

Chaikin, Miriam. *A Nightmare in History: The Holocaust 1933–1945*. New York: Ticknor & Fields, 1987.

Dabringhaus, Erhard. *Klaus Barbie*. Washington, D.C.: Acropolis Books Ltd., 1984.

Eisner, Jack. *The Survivor*. New York: William Morrow and Company, Inc., 1980.

Epstein, Helen. *Children of the Holocaust*. New York: G. P. Putnam's Sons, 1979.

Facing History and Ourselves Holocaust and Human Behavior Resource Book. Brookline, Mass.: Facing History and Ourselves National Foundation, Inc., 1994.

Frank, Anne. *Anne Frank: The Diary of a Young Girl*. Garden City, N.Y.: Doubleday, 1967.

Gilbert, Martin. *The Holocaust: A History of the Jews of Europe during the Second World War*. New York: Henry Holt, 1985.

Gill, Anton. *The Journey Back from Hell*. New York: William Morrow, 1988.

Grant, Neil. *The Partition of Palestine, 1947*. New York: Franklin Watts, 1973.

Greenfield, Howard. *The Hidden Children*. New York: Ticknor & Fields, 1993.

Korn, Abram. *Abe's Story: A Holocaust Memoir*. Atlanta, Ga.: Longstreet Press, 1995.

Landau, Ronnie. *The Nazi Holocaust*. Chicago: Ivan R. Dee, 1994.

Leckie, Robert. *Delivered from Evil: The Saga of World War II*. New York: Harper & Row Publishers, 1987.

Levy, Alan. *The Wiesenthal File*. Grand Rapids, Mich.: William B. Eerdmans Publishing Company, 1993.

Neave, Airey. *Nuremberg: A Personal Record of the Trial of the Major Nazi War Criminals in 1945-6*. London: Hodder and Stoughton, 1978.

Noble, Iris. *Nazi Hunter: Simon Wiesenthal*. New York: Julian Messner, 1979.

Oliner, Samuel P., and Pearl M. Oliner. *The Altruistic Personality*. New York: The Free Press, 1988.

Persico, Joseph E. *Nuremberg: Infamy on Trial*. New York: Penguin Books, 1994.

Sachar, Howard M. *A History of Israel from the Rise of Zionism to our Time*. New York: Alfred A. Knopf, 1996.

Scharfstein, Sol. *Understanding Israel*. Hoboken, N.J.: KTAV Publishing House, Inc., 1994.

Sichrovsky, Peter. *Born Guilty*. New York: Basic Books, Inc., 1988.

———. *Strangers in Their Own Land*. New York: Basic Books, 1986.

Simpson, Christopher. *Blowback*. New York: Weidenfeld & Nicolson, 1988.

Terkel, Studs. *The Good War: An Oral History of World War Two*. New York: Ballantine Books, 1984.

Wardi, Dina. *Memorial Candles*. London: Routledge, 1992.

Wiesel, Elie. *Night*. New York: Bantam Books, 1982.

Wilson, Cara. *Love, Otto: The Legacy of Anne Frank*. Kansas City: Andrews and McMeel, 1995.

INDEX